SOCIAL LIFE IN
OLD NEW ORLEANS

THE AUTHOR AT TWENTY-TWO

Painted by Moïse

SOCIAL LIFE IN OLD NEW ORLEANS

Being Recollections of my Girlhood

BY

ELIZA RIPLEY

ILLUSTRATED

A FIREBIRD PRESS BOOK

PELICAN PUBLISHING COMPANY
Gretna 1998

Manufactured in the United States of America

Published by Pelican Publishing Company, Inc.
1000 Burmaster Street, Gretna, Louisiana 70053

To
MY CHILDREN
and
MY CHILDREN'S CHILDREN
and to
THEIR CHILDREN TO COME

FOREWORD

Far more vivid than the twilight of the days in which I dwell, there rises before my inner eye the vision, aglow in Southern sunshine, of the days that are gone, never to return, but which formed the early chapters of a life that has been lived, that can never be lived again.

Many of the following stories are oft-told tales at my fireside—others were written to record phases of the patriarchal existence before the war which has so utterly passed away.

They have been printed from time to time in the pages of the New Orleans *Times-Democrat*, the editor of which has very kindly consented to their publication in this form.

CONTENTS

CONTENTS

LIST OF ILLUSTRATIONS

SOCIAL LIFE IN OLD NEW ORLEANS

I

NEW ORLEANS CHILDREN OF 1840

CHILDREN should be seen and not heard."
Children were neither seen nor heard in
the days of which I write, the days of
1840. They led the simple life, going and coming in their own unobtrusive way, making no stir
in fashionable circles, with laces and flounces and
feathered hats. There were no ready-made garments then for grown-ups, much less for children.
It was before California gold mines, before the
Mexican war, before money was so abundant that
we children could turn up our little noses at a
picayune. I recall the time when Alfred Munroe
descended from Boston upon the mercantile world
of New Orleans, and opened on Camp Street a
"one price" clothing store for men. Nobody had
ever heard of one price, and no deviation, for
anything, from a chicken to a plantation. The fun

of hectoring over price, and feeling, no matter how the trade ended, you had a bargain after all, was denied the customers of Mr. Alfred Munroe. The innovation was startling, but Munroe retired with a fortune in course of time.

Children's clothes were homemade. A little wool shawl for the shoulders did duty for common use. A pelisse made out of an old one of mother's, or some remnant found in the house, was fine for Sunday wear. Pantalettes of linen, straight and narrow and untrimmed, fell over our modest little legs to our very shoetops. Our dresses were equally simple and equally "cut down and made over." Pantalettes were white, but I recall, with a dismal smile, that when I was put into what might be called unmitigated mourning for a brother, my pantalettes matched my dresses, black bombazine or black alpaca.

Our amusements were of the simplest. My father's house on Canal Street had a flat roof, well protected by parapets, so it furnished a grand playground for the children of the neighborhood. Judge Story lived next door and Sid and Ben Story enjoyed to the full the advantages of that roof, where all could romp and jump rope to their heart's content. The neutral ground, that is now a center for innumerable lines of street cars, was at that time an open, ungarnished, untrimmed, untended strip of waste land. An Italian banana and orange man cleared a space among the bushes and rank weeds and erected a rude fruit stall where later Clay's statue stood. A quadroon woman had a coffee stand, in the early mornings, at the next corner, opposite my father's house. It could not have been much beyond Claiborne Street that we children went crawfishing in the ditches that bounded each side of that neutral ground, for we walked, and it was not considered far.

The Farmers' and Traders' Bank was on Canal Street, and the family of Mr. Bell, the cashier, lived over the bank. There were children there and a governess, who went fishing with us. We rarely caught anything and had no use for it when we did.

Sometimes I was permitted to go to market with John, way down to the old French Market. We had to start early, before the shops on Chartres Street were open, and the boys busy with scoops watered the roadway from brimming gutters. John and I hurried past. Once at market we rushed from stall to stall, filling our basket, John forgetting nothing that had been ordered, and always carefully remembering one most important item, the saving of at least a picayune out of the market money for a cup of coffee at Manette's stall. I drank half the coffee and took one of the little cakes. John finished the repast and "dreened" the cup, and with the remark, "We won't say anything about this," we started toward home. We had to stop, though, at a bird store, on the square above the Cathedral, look at the birds, chaff the noisy parrots, watch the antics of the monkeys, and see the man hang up his strings of corals and fix his shells in the window, ready for the day's business. We could scarcely tear ourselves away, it was so interesting; but a reminder that the wax head at Dr. De Leon's dentist's door would be "put out by this time," hurried me to see that wonderful bit of mechanism open and shut its mouth, first with a row of teeth, then revealing an empty cavern. How I watched, wondered and admired that awfully artificial wax face! These occasional market trips—and walks with older members of the family—were the sum of my or any other child's recreation

Once, and only once, there was a party! The little Maybins had a party and every child I knew was invited. The Maybins lived somewhere back of Poydras Market. I recall we had to walk down Poydras Street, beyond the market, and turn to the right onto a street that perhaps had a name, but I never heard it.

The home was detached, and surrounded by

ample grounds; quantities of fig trees, thickets of running roses and in damp places clusters of palmetto and blooming flags. We little invited guests were promptly on the spot at 4 P. M., and as promptly off the spot at early candlelight. I am sure no débutantes ever had a better time than did we little girls in pantalettes and pigtails. We danced; Miss Sarah Strawbridge played for us, and we all knew how to dance. Didn't we belong to Mme. Arraline Brooks' dancing school?

The corner of Camp and Julia Streets, diagonally across from the then fashionable 13 Buildings, was occupied by Mme. Arraline Brooks, a teacher of dancing. Her school (studio or parlor it would be called now) was on the second floor of Armory Hall, and there we children—she had an immense class, too—learned all the fancy whirls and "heel and toe" steps of the intricate polka, which was danced in sets of eight, like old-time quadrilles. Mme. Arraline wore in the classroom short skirts and pantalettes, so we had a good sight of her feet as she pirouetted about, as agile as a ballet dancer.

By and by, at a signal from Miss Sarah, who had been having a confidential and persuasive interview with a little miss, we were all placed with our backs to the wall and a space cleared. Miss Sarah struck a few notes, and little Tenie Slocomb danced the "Highland fling." Very beautiful was the little sylph in white muslin, her short sleeves tied with blue ribbons, and she so graceful and lovely. It comes to me to-day with a thrill, when I compare the companion picture—of a pale, delicate, dainty old lady, with silvered hair and tottering step, on the bank of a foreign river. It is not easy to bridge the seventy years (such a short span, too, it is) between the two. Then the march from "Norma" started us to the room for refreshments. It is full forty years since I have heard that old familiar air, but for thirty years after that date I did not hear it that the impulse to march to lemonade and sponge cake did not seize me.

Alack-a-day! Almost all of us have marched away.

II

NEW ORLEANS SCHOOLS AND TEACHERS IN THE FORTIES

OF course, seventy years ago, as in the ages past and to come, convents were the places for educating young girls in a Catholic community. Nevertheless, there have always been schools and schools, for those whom it was not expedient or convenient to board in a convent. In New Orleans the Ursuline Convent was too remote from the majority of homes for these day scholars, so there were a few schools among the many that come to my mind to-day, not that I ever entered one of them, but I had girl friends in all. In the thirties St. Angelo had a school on Customhouse Street, next door to the home of the Zacharies. His method of teaching may have been all right, but his discipline was objectionable; he had the delinquent pupils kneel on brickdust and tacks and there study aloud the neglected lesson. Now, brickdust isn't so very bad, and tacks only a trifle worse, when one's knees are protected by stockings or even pantalettes, but stockings in those days did not extend over the knee, and old St. Angelo was sure to see that the pantalettes were well rolled up. This method of discipline was not acceptable to parents whose children came home with bruises and wounds. That dominie retired from business before the forties.

Mme. Granet had a school for girls in the French municipality. Elinor Longer, one of my most intimate friends, attended it, and she used to tell us stories that convulsed us with laughter about Madame's daughter. Lina had some eye trouble, and was forbidden to "exercise the tear glands," but her tears flowed copiously when Madame refused to submit to her freaks. Thus Lina managed, in a way, to run the school, having half holidays and other indulgences so dear to the schoolgirl, at her own sweet will.

At the haunted house (I wonder if it is still standing and still haunted?) on Royal Street, Mme. Delarouelle had a school for *demoiselles*. Rosa, daughter of Judge John M. Duncan, was a scholar there. I don't think the madame had any boarders, though the house was large and commodious, even if it was haunted by ghosts of maltreated negroes. The school could not under those circumstances have continued many years, for every child knew it was dangerous to cross its portals. Our John told

8

me he "seed a skel'ton hand" clutching the grated front door once, and he never walked on that side of the street thereafter. He even knew a man "dat seen eyes widout sockets or sockets widout eyes, he dun know which, but dey could see, all de same, and they was a looken out'en one of the upstairs winders." With such gruesome talk many a child was put to bed in my young days.

Doctor, afterward Bishop Hawks, when he was rector of Christ Church, then on Canal Street, had a school on Girod Street. It was a temporary affair and did not continue over a season or two. It was entirely conducted by Mrs. Hawks and her daughters, so far as I know, for, as before mentioned, I attended none of the schools.

In 1842 there was a class in Spanish at Mr. Hennen's house, on Royal Street, near Canal. Señor Marino Cubi y Soler was the teacher of that class; a very prosaic and painstaking teacher he was, too, notwithstanding his startlingly high flown cognomen. Miss Anna Maria and young Alfred Hennen and a Dr. Rhodes, from the Belize, as the mouth of the Mississippi is called, with a few other grown-ups, formed the señor's class. I was ten years old, but was allowed to join with some other members of my family, though my mother protested it was nonsense for a child like me and a waste of money.

9

Father did not agree with her, and after over sixty years to think it over, I don't either. When the señor's class dispersed I imagine the text-books, of which, by the way, he was author, were laid aside. But years and years thereafter, during the war, while traveling in Mexico, some of the señor's teaching came miraculously back to me, bringing with it enough Spanish to be of material help in that stranger country.

Another teacher wandered from house to house with his "Telemaque" and "colloquial phrases," giving lessons in French. Gimarchi, from the name, may have been partly, at least, Italian, but he was a fine teacher of the sister language. *Por supuésto,* his itinerary was confined to the American district of the city.

Is it any surprise that the miscellaneous education we girls of seventy years ago in New Orleans had access to, culminated by fitting us for housewives and mothers, instead of writers and platform speakers, doctors and lawyers—suffragettes? Everybody was musical; every girl had music lessons and every mother superintended the study and practice of the one branch deemed absolutely indispensable to the education of a *demoiselle*. The city was dotted all over with music teachers, but Mme. Boyer was, par excellence, the most popular. She did not wander

RICHARD HENRY CHINN
Painted by Hardin

from house to house, but the *demoiselles,* music roll in hand, repaired to her domicile, and received instruction in a music room barely large enough to contain a piano, a scholar and a madame who was, to say the least, immense in bulk, the style of Creole who appears best in a black silk *blouse volante.*

Art was not taught, art was not studied, art was not appreciated. I mean by art the pencil and the brush, so busily wielded in every school now. No doubt there were stifled geniuses whose dormant talent was never suspected, so utterly ignored were the brush and the palette of the lover of art. I call to mind the ability evinced by Miss Celestine Eustis in the use of the pencil. She occasionally gave a friend a glimpse of some of her work, of which, I regret to say, she was almost ashamed, not of the work, but of the doing it. I recall a sketch taken of Judge Eustis' balcony, and a group of young society men; the likenesses, unmistakably those of George Eustis and of Destour Foucher, were striking.

M. Devoti, with his violin in a green baize bag, was a professor of deportment and dancing. He undertook to train two gawky girls of the most awkward age in my father's parlor. M. Devoti wore corsets! and laced, as the saying is, "within an inch of his life." He wore a long-tail coat, very full at the spider waist-line, that hung all round him, almost to the knees, so he used it like a woman's skirt, and could demonstrate to the awkward girls the art of holding out their skirts with thumb and forefinger, and all the other fingers sticking out stiff and straight. Then curtsey! throw out the right foot, draw up the left.

Another important branch of deportment was to seat the awkwards stiffly on the extreme edge of a chair, fold the hands on the very precarious lap, droop the eyes in a pensive way. Then Devoti would flourish up and present, with an astonishing salaam, a book from the center table. The young miss was instructed how to rise, bow and receive the book, in the most affected and mechanical style. Another exercise was to curtsey, accept old Devoti's arm and majestically parade round and round the center table. The violin emerged from the baize bag, Devoti made it screech a few notes while the trio balanced up and down, changed partners and promenaded, till the awkwards were completely bewildered and tired out. He then replaced the violin, made a profound bow to extended skirts and curtseys, admonished the pupils to practice for next lesson, and vanished. Thus ended the first lesson. Dear me! Pock-marked, spider-waist Devoti is as plain to my eye to-day as he was in the flesh, bowing, smiling, dancing with flourishing steps as in the days of long ago.

Were those shy girls benefited by that artificial training? I opine not. This seems to modern eyes, mayhap, a whimsical exaggeration; nevertheless, it is a true picture. Devoti's style was indeed the "end of an era"; he had no successor. Turveydrop, the immortal Turveydrop himself, was not even an imitator. These old schools and teachers march before my mind's eye to-day; very vivid it all is to me, though the last of them, and perhaps all those they tried to teach, have passed away. Children who went to Mme. Granet and Mme. Delarouelle and Dr. Hawks and all the other schools of that day, sent their daughters, a decade or two later, to Mme. Desrayoux. Now she is gone and many of the daughters gone also. And it is left to one old lady to dig out the past, and recall, possibly to no one but herself, New Orleans schools, teachers and scholars of seventy years ago.

III

BOARDING SCHOOL IN THE FORTIES

I WONDER if the parents of the present do not sometimes contrast the fashionable schools in which their daughters are being educated with the fashionable schools to which their aged mothers, mayhap grandmothers, were sent sixty and more years ago? Among my possessions that I keep—according to the dictum of my grandchildren—"for sentimental sake," is a much-worn "Scholar's Companion," which they scorn to look at when I bring it forth, and explain it to be the best speller that ever was; and a bent, much overworked crochet needle of my schooldays, for we worked with our hands as well as with our brains. The boarding school to which I refer was not unique, but a typical New England seminary of the forties. It was both fashionable and popular, but the young ladies were not, as now, expected to appear at a 6 o'clock dinner in a low neck (oh, my!) gown.

Lately, passing through the now much expanded city to which I was sent, such a young girl, on a sailing ship from New Orleans to New York in the early spring of 1847, I spent a half hour walking on Crown Street looking for No. 111. It was not there, not a trace of the building of my day left; nor was one, so far as I know, of the girls, my old schoolmates, left; all three of the dear, painstaking teachers sleeping in the old cemetery, at rest at last were they. Every blessed one lives in my memory, bright and young, patient and middle-aged—all are here to beguile my twilight hours. . . . .

The school routine was simple and precise, especially the latter. We had duties outside the schoolroom, the performance of which was made pleasant and acceptable, as when the freshly laundered clothes were stacked in neat little piles on the long table of the yellow room on Thursdays, ready for each girl to carry to her own room. There were also neat little stacks on each girl's desk, of personal articles requiring repairs, buttons to replace, holes to patch, stockings to darn, and in the schoolroom on Thursday afternoons—how some of us hated the work!—it was examined and passed upon before we were dismissed. The long winter evenings we were assembled in the library and one of the teachers read to us. I remember one winter we had "Guy Mannering" and "Quentin Durward," Sir Walter Scott's lovely stories. We girls were expected to bring some work to occupy our fingers while listening to the readings, with the comments and explanations that illuminated obscure portions we might not comprehend.

There was an old-fashioned "high boy" (*haut bois*) in the library, in the capacious drawers of which were unmade garments for the missionary box. Woe unto the young lady who had no knitting, crocheting or hemstitching of her own to do! She could sew on red flannel for the little Hottentots! After hymn singing Sunday afternoons there was reading from some suitably saintly book. We had "Keith's Evidences of Prophecy" (I have not seen a copy of that much-read and laboriously explained volume for more than sixty years). The tension of our minds produced by "prophecy" was mitigated once in a while by two goody-goody books, "Lamton Parsonage" and "Amy Herbert," both, no doubt, long out of print.

There also were stately walks to be taken twice a day for recreation; walks down on the "Strand," or some back street that led away from college campus and flirtatious students. Our school happened to be too near the college green, by the way. We marched in couples, a teacher to lead who had eyes both before and behind, and a teacher similarly equipped to follow. With all these precautions we—some of us were pretty—were often convulsed beyond bounds when "we met by chance, the only way," on the very backest street, a procession of college fellows on mischief bent, marching two and two, just like us. In bad weather we were shod with what were called "gums" and wrapped in coats long and shaggy and weighing a ton. Waterproofs were a later invention. Wet or dry, cold or warm, those exercises had to be taken to keep us in good physical condition. I must mention in this connection that no matter what ailed us, in stomach or back, head or foot, we were dosed with hot ginger tea. I do not remember ever seeing a doctor in the house, or knowing of one being summoned. The girls hated that ginger tea, so no doubt many an incipient headache was not reported.

With the four spinsters (we irreverently called No. 111 Old Maids' Hall) who lived in the house, there were scraggly, baldheaded, spectacled teachers from outside—a monsieur who read Racine and Molière with us and taught us *j'aime, tu aime,* which he could safely do, the snuffy old man; a fatherly sort of Turveydrop dancing master, who cracked our feet with his fiddle bow; a drawing master, who, because he sometimes led his class on sketching trips up Hillhouse Avenue, was immensely popular, and every one of us wanted to take drawing lessons. We did some water colors, too; some of us had not one particle of artistic talent. I was one of that sort, but I achieved a Baltimore oriole, which, years after, my admiring husband, who also had no artistic taste, had framed and "hung on the line" in our hall. Perhaps some Yankee may own it now, for during the war they took everything else we had, and surely a brilliant Baltimore oriole did not escape their rapacity!

Solid English branches were taught by the dear spinsters. We did not skin cats and dissect them. There was no class in anatomy, but there was a botany class, and we dissected wild flowers, which is a trifle more ladylike. Our drilling in chirography was something to marvel at in these days when the young people affect such complicated and involved handwriting that is not easily decipherable. And grammar! I now slip up in both grammar and rhetoric, but I have arrived at the failing age. We spent the greater part of a session parsing Pope's "Essay on Man," and at the closing of that book I think we knew the whole thing by heart. Discipline was, so to say, honorary. There were rules as to study and practice hours, and various other things. Saturday morning, after the "Collect of the day" and prayers, when we were presumed to be in a celestial frame of mind, each girl reported her infringement of rules—if she was delinquent, and she generally was. That system served to make us more truthful and conscientious than some of us might have been under a different training.

It was expressly stipulated that no money be furnished the pupils. A teacher accompanied us to do necessary shopping and used her discretion in the selection. If one of us expressed the need of new shoes her entire stock was inspected, and if a pair could be repaired it was done and the purchase postponed. Now, bear in mind, this was not a cheap, second rate school, but one of the best known and most fashionable. There were several young ladies from the South among the twenty or so boarders. The Northern girls were from the prominent New York families—Shermans, Kirbys, Phalens, Pumpellys and Thorns. This was before the fashionables of to-day came to the fore.

Speaking of reporting our delinquencies, we knew quite well that it was against the custom, at least, to bring reading matter into the school. There was a grand, large library of standard works of merit at our free disposal. In some way "Jane Eyre" (just published) was smuggled in and we were secretly reading it by turns. How the spinsters found it out we never knew, but they always found out everything, so we were scarcely surprised one Saturday morning to receive a lecture on the pernicious character of the book "Jane Eyre," so unlike (and alas! so much more interesting than) Amy Herbert, with her missionary basket, her coals and her flannel petticoats. We were questioned, not by wholesale, but individually, if we had the book? If we had read the book? The first two or three in the row could reply in the negative, but as interrogations ran down the line toward the guilty ones they were all greatly relieved when one brave girl replied, "Yes, ma'am, I am almost through, please let me finish it." Then "Jane" vanished from our possession.

When the Church Sewing Society met at our house, certain girls who were sufficiently advanced in music to afford entertainment to the guests were summoned to the parlor to play and sing, and incidentally have a lemonade and a jumble. I was the star performer (had I not been a pupil of Cripps, Dr. Clapp's organist, since I was able to reach the pedal with my foot?). My overture of "La Dame Blanche" was quite a masterpiece, but my "Battle of Prague" was simply stunning. The "advance," the "rattle of musketry," the "beating of drums" (did you ever see the music score?) I could render with such force that the dear, busy ladies almost jumped from their seats. There were two Kentucky girls with fine voices also invited to entertain the guests. Alas! our fun came to an end. On one occasion when I ended the "Battle of Prague" with a terrific bang, there was an awful moment of silence, when one of the ladies sneezed with such unexpected force that her false teeth careered clear across the room! Not one of the guests saw it, or was aware that she quietly walked over and replaced them, but we naughty girls were so brimful of fun that we exploded with laughter. Nothing was said to us of the unfortunate contretemps, but the musical programmes were discontinued.

College boys helped to make things lively for us, though we did not have bowing acquaintance with one of them. Valentines poured in to us; under doors and over fences they rained. The dear spinsters laughed over them with us. Thanksgiving morning, when the front door was opened for the first time, and we were assembled in the hall ready to march to 11 o'clock church service, a gaunt, skinny, starved-to-death turkey was found suspended to the door knob, conspicuously tied by a broad red ribbon, with a Thanksgiving greeting painted on, so "one who ran could read." No doubt a good many had read and run, for there had been hours allowed them. The dear spinsters were so mortified and shocked that we girls had not the courage to laugh.

By reason of my distance from home, reached by a long voyage on a sailing ship—the first steamer service between New York and New Orleans was in the autumn of 1848, and the Crescent City was the pioneer steamer—I spent the vacations under the benign influence of the teachers, always the only girl left, but busy and happy, enjoying all the privileges of a parlor boarder. I still have a book full of written directions for knitting and crocheting, and making all sorts of old-timey needle books and pincushions, the initial directions dated 1846, largely the collection and record of more than one long summer vacation at that New England school. What girl of to-day would submit to such training and routine? What boarding school, seminary or college is to-day conducted on such lines? Not one that you or I know. The changes in everything, in every walk of life, from the simple in my day and generation to the complicated of the present, sets me to moralizing. Like all old people who are not able to take an active interest in the present, I live in the past, where the disappointments and heartaches, for surely we must have had our share, are forgotten. We old people live in the atmosphere of a day dead—and gone—and glorified!

IV

THE first time I ever saw a penny was at school in Yankeeland in 1847. It was given me to pay the man for bringing me a letter from the postoffice—10 cents postage, 1 cent delivery, in those days. People had to get their mail at the office. There was no free delivery. Certain neighborhoods of spinsters, however—the college town was full of such—secured the services of a lame, halt or blind man to bring their letters from the office to their door once a day for the stipend of a penny each.

There was no coin in circulation of less value than a picayune where was my home. A picayune, which represented so little value that a miser was called picayunish, at the same time represented such a big value that we children felt rich when we had one tied in the corner of our handkerchief. At the corner of Chartres and Canal Streets was a tiny soda fountain, where one could get a glass of soda for a picayune—or mead. We children liked mead. I never see it now, but, as I recall, it was a thick, honey, creamy drink. We must have preferred it because it seemed so much more for a picayune than the frothy, effervescent, palish soda water. It was a great lark to go with Pa and take my glass of mead, while he ordered ginger syrup (of all things!) with his soda. The changing years bring gold

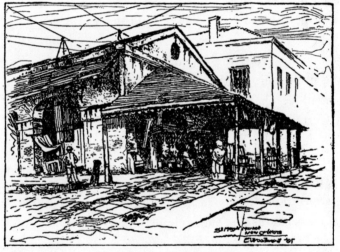

MARKET DOORWAY.

mines, greenbacks, tariffs, labor exactions and *nouveaux riches,* and a penny now buys about what a picayune did in my day. One pays a penny for ever so big a newspaper to-day. A picayune was the price of a small sheet in my time.

Many of us must remember the colored *mar-*

chandes who walked the street with trays, deftly balanced on their heads, arms akimbo, calling out their dainties, which were in picayune piles on the trays—six small celesto figs, or five large blue ones, nestling on fig leaves; lovely popcorn tic tac balls made with that luscious "open kettle" sugar, that dear, fragrant brown sugar no one sees now. Pralines with the same sugar; why, we used it in our coffee. A few years ago, visiting dear Mrs. Ida Richardson, I reveled in our breakfast coffee. "I hope you preserve your taste for brown sugar coffee?" she said. I fairly jumped at the treat.

But a *marchande* is passing up the street, and if I am a little girl, I beg a picayune for a praline; if I am an old lady, I invest a picayune in a leaf with six *figues celestes*. Mme. Chose—I don't give any more definite name, for it is a sub rosa venture on her part—had a soirée last night. Madame buys her *chapeaux* of Olympe, and her *toilettes* from Pluche or Ferret, and if her home is way down, even below Esplanade Street, where many Creoles live, she is thrifty and frugal. So this morning a chocolate-colored *marchande*, who usually vends picayune bouquets of violets from madame's *parterre*, has her tray filled with picayune stacks of broken nougat pyramid and candied orange and macaroons very daintily arranged on bits of tissue paper. I vividly recall encountering way down Royal Street, where no one was loitering to see me, this chocolate *marchande,* and recognizing the delicacies of a ball the previous night. I was on my way to call on Mrs. Garnet Duncan, the dear, delightful woman who was such a *gourmande,* and I knew how delicious were those sweets; no one could excel a Creole madame in this confection. So I invested a few picayunes in some of the most attractive, carrying off to my sweet friend what I conveniently could. How she did enjoy them! And how she complained I had not brought more! The *mesdames* of that date are gone; gone also, no doubt, are the *marchandes* they sent forth. It was a very picayunish sort of business, but labor did not count, for one was not paying $20 a month for the reluctant services of a chocolate lady.

Then again, in the early morning, when one, *en papilottes,* came down to breakfast, listless and "out of sorts," the chant of the cream cheese woman would be heard. A rush to the door with a saucer for a cheese, a tiny, heart-shaped cheese, a dash of cream poured from a claret bottle over it—all this for a picayune! How nice and refreshing it was. What a glorious addition to the breakfast that promised to pall on one's appetite.

Picayune was the standard coin at the market. I

wonder what is now? Soup bone was *un escalin* (two picayunes), but one paid for the soup vegetables, a bit of cabbage, a leek, a sprig of parsley, a tiny carrot, a still tinier turnip, all tied in a slender package. A *cornet* of fresh gumbo *filé,* a bunch of horse-radish roots, a little sage, parsley, herbs of every sort in packages and piles, a string of dried grasshoppers for the mocking bird, *"un picayun,"* the Indian or black woman squatting on the *banquette* at the old French Market would tell you.

A picayune was the smallest coin the richly appareled madame or the poor market negro could put in the collection box as she paused on her way at the Cathedral to tell her beads. There was no occasion for the priest to rebuke his flock for niggardliness. They may have been picayunish, but not to the extent of the congregation of one of the largest Catholic churches I wot of to-day, where the fathers were so tired counting pennies that it was announced from the pulpit: "No more pennies must be put in the box. We spend hours every week counting and stacking pennies, and it is a shocking waste of time. If you are so destitute that you can't afford at least a nickel to your church, come to the vestry, after mass, and we will look into your needs and give you the relief the church always extends to her poor."

The shabby old negro, with her heavy market basket, returning home, no doubt needing the prayers of her patron saint or some other churchly office, filched the picayune from the carefully counted market money. I know, no matter how carefully my mother doled the market fund to John, he always contrived to secure a picayune out of it, and for no saint, either, but for old Coffee-stand Palmyre.

Do not we old ladies remember the picayune dolls of our childhood? The wooden jointed dolls, the funny little things we had to play with, every feature, even hair and yellow earrings, painted on little, smooth bullet heads. They could be made to sit down and to crook their arms, but no ingenuity could make them stand a-loney. How we loved those little wooden dolls! We do not see a pauper child, not even a poor little blackie, with a picayune doll nowadays. I really believe we—I am talking of old ladies now—were happier, and had more fun with our picayune family than the little girls of the present day have with their $10 dolls, with glass eyes that are sure to fall out and long curls that are sure to tangle. We had no fears about the eyes and hair of our picayunes.

The picayune, whose memory I invoke, was a Spanish coin, generally worn pretty thin and often having a small hole in it. I remember my ambition was to accumulate enough picayunes to string on a thread for an ornament. It is unnecessary to say that in those thrifty days my ambition was not gratified. It is more than fifty years since I have seen one of those old 6¼ cent picayunes. I have a stiff, wooden corset board that I sometimes take out to show to my granddaughter when I find her "stooping," that she may see the instrument that made grandma so straight. I would like to have a picayune to add to my very limited collection of relics. They flourished at the same era and have together vanished from our homes and shops.

We all must have known some "picayune people." There was a family living near us who owned and occupied a large, fine home on St. Joseph Street, while we and the Grimshaws and Beins lived in rented houses near by. They had, besides, a summer home "over the lake" (and none of us had!). Often, on Mondays, a fish, or a quart of shrimp, or something else in the "over the lake" line, was sent to one of us, for sale. We used to laugh over the littleness of the thing. A quart of shrimp for a picayune was cheap and tempting, but none of us cared to buy of our rich neighbor. The climax came when an umbrella went the rounds for inspection. It was for raffle! Now, umbrellas, like pocket handkerchiefs, are always useful and never go out of fashion. With one accord, we declined chances in the umbrella.

I feel I am, for the fun of the thing, dragging forth a few skeletons from closets, but I do not ticket them, so no harm is done. In fact, if I ever knew, I have long since forgotten the name to tack onto the umbrella skeleton. And the fashionable madame who sent out on the streets what a lady we knew called the "perquisites" of her soirée supper has left too many well-known descendants. I would scorn to ticket the skeleton of that frugal and thrifty madame. There are no more umbrellas for a picayunish skeleton to raffle, no more such delicious sweets for the madame to stack into picayune piles, and, alack-a-day! no more picayunes, either.

V

HOUSEKEEPING is vastly simplified since the days when my mother washed her teacups and spoons every morning. I love the old way; however, I do not practise it. If my grandchildren were to see the little wooden piggin brought me on a tray after breakfast, and see me wash the silver and glass they would think grandma has surely lost her mind. That purely domestic housewifely habit lasted long after my mother had passed away. It still is the vogue in many a New England household, but no doubt is among the lost virtues South. When I was a young lady and occasionally (oh, happy times!) spent a few days with the Slocombs, I always saw Mrs. Slocomb and her aged mother, dear old Mrs. Cox, who tremblingly loved to help, pass the tea things through their own delicate hands every morning. So it was at Mrs. Leonard Matthews', and so it was in scores of wealthy homes.

Though we had ever so many servants, our family being a large one, my semi-invalid mother, who rarely left her home and never made visits, did a thousand little household duties that are now, even in families where only one or two servants are kept, entirely ignored by the ladies of the house. After a dinner party or an evening entertainment, and my father was hospitably inclined—much beyond his means—my mother passed all the silver, glass and china through her own delicate fingers, and we did not, as I recall after all this lapse of years, have anything of superlative value. It was not a matter of thrift or economy on her part, but a matter of course; everybody did the same.

After a visit to a New England family several years ago I was telling a Creole friend of the lovely old India china that had been in daily use over three generations. The reply was: "Oh, but they did not have a Christophe." No doubt they had had several Christophes, but they never had a chance to wash those valuable cups. In the days of long ago housewives did not have negligées with floating ribbons and smart laces. They had calico gowns that a splash of water could not ruin.

Household furniture—I go back full seventy years—was simple and easily cared for. Carpets were generally what was known as "three-ply." I don't see them now, but in places, on humble

A New Orleans Yard and Cistern.

floors, I see imitation Brussels or some other counterfeit. The first carpet I ever saw woven in one
piece, like all the rugs so plentiful now (and that
was at a much later date) was on the parlor floor of
the Goodman house, on Toulouse Street, the home
so full of bright young girls I so loved to visit.
There was no concern to take away carpets to be
cleaned and stored in the summer. Carpets were
taken to some vacant lot and well beaten. The
neutral green on Canal Street, green and weedy it
was, too, was a grand place to shake carpets; no
offense given if one carried them beyond Claiborne
Street where were no pretentious houses. Then
those carpets were thickly strewn with tobacco
leaves, rolled up and stored in the garret, if you
had one. Every house did not boast of that convenience.

Curtains were not satin damask. At the Mint
when Joe Kennedy was superintendent, and his
family were fashionable people, their parlor curtains were some red cotton stuff, probably what
is known as turkey red; there was a white and
red-figured border; they were looped over
gilt rods meant to look like spears and muskets,
in deference, I suppose, to the military side of
that government building, for there were senti-
nels and guards stationed around about that

gave the whole concern a most imposing and military air.

I remember at the Breedloves' home there were net curtains (probably mosquito net), with a red border. They were thought rather novel and stylish. There were no madras, no Irish point, no Nottingham curtains even, so one did not have a large variety to choose from.

People had candelabras, and some elaborate affairs—they called them girandoles—to hold candles; they had heavy crystal drops that tinkled and scintillated and were prismatic and on the whole were rather fine. The candles in those gorgeous stands and an oil lamp on the inevitable center-table were supposed to furnish abundance of light for any occasion. When my sister dressed for a function she had two candles to dress by (so did I ten years later!), and two dusky maids to follow her all about, and hold them at proper points so the process of the toilet could be satisfactorily accomplished. Two candles without shades—nobody had heard of shades—were sufficient for an ordinary tea table. I was a grown girl, fresh from school, when I saw the first gaslight in a private house, at Mrs. Slocomb's, on St. Charles Street. People sewed, embroidered, read and wrote and played chess evenings by candlelight, and except a few near-sighted people and the aged no one used glasses. There was not an oculist (a specialist, I mean) in the whole city.

Every woman had to sew. There were well-trained seamstresses in every house; no "ready-mades," no machines. Imagine the fine hand-sewing on shirt bosoms, collars and cuffs. I can hear my mother's voice now, "Be careful in the stitching of that bosom; take up two and skip four," which I early learned meant the threads of the linen. What a time there was when the boys grew to tailor-cut pantaloons! Cut by a tailor, sewed at home, what a to-do there was when Charley had his first tail-coat; he could not sit on the tails, they were too short, so he made an uproar.

I recall also how I cried when sister's old red and black "shot silk" dress was made over for me, and I thought I was going to be so fine (I was nine years old then and was beginning to "take notice"). The goods fell short, and I had to have a black, low neck, short-sleeve waist. In vain I was told it was velvet and ever so stylish and becoming. I knew better. However, that abbreviated dress and those abbreviated tails did duty at the dancing school.

But we have wandered from house furnishings to children's clothes. We will go upstairs now and take a look at the ponderous four-poster bed, with its awful tester top, that covered it like a flat roof. That tester was ornamented with a wall paper stuff, a wreath of impossible red and yellow roses, big as saucers, stamped on it, and four strands of same roses reaching to the four corners of the monstrosity. The idea of lying, with a raging fever or a splitting headache, under such a canopy! However, there were "swells" (there always are "swells") who had testers covered with silk.

I hear a rumor that furniture covered with horsehair cloth is about to come to the fore again. Everybody in my early day had black haircloth furniture; maybe that was one reason red curtains were preferred, for furniture covered with black haircloth was fearfully funereal. However, as no moth devoured it, dust did not rest on its slick, shiny surface, and it lasted forever, it had its advantages. Every household possessed a haircloth sofa, with a couple of hard, round pillows of the same, the one too slippery to nap on and the others regular breaknecks.

Butler's pantry! My stars! Who ever heard of a butler's pantry, and sinks, and running water, and faucets inside houses? The only running water was a hydrant in the yard; the only sink was the gutter in the yard; the sewer was the gutter in the

Door in the French Market

DOOR IN THE FRENCH MARKET

street, so why a butler's pantry? To be sure there was a cistern for rainwater, and jars like those Ali Baba's forty thieves hid themselves in. Those earthen jars were replenished from the hydrant, and the muddy river water "settled" by the aid of almond hulls or alum.

Of course, every house had a storeroom, called pantry, to hold supplies. It was lined with shelves, but the only light and air was afforded by a half-moon aperture cut into a heavy batten door. We had wire safes on the back porch and a zinc-lined box for the ice—nothing else—wrapped in a gray blanket, gray, I presume, on the same principle we children preferred pink cocoanut cakes—they kept clean longer than the white! Ice was in general use but very expensive. It was brought by ship from the North, in hogsheads.

For the kitchen there were open fireplaces with a pot hanging from a crane, skillets and spiders. We don't even hear the names of those utensils now. By and by an enterprising housewife ventured on a cook stove. I have a letter written by one such, dated in New Orleans in 1840, in which she descants on the wonders achieved by her stove. "Why, Susan, we baked three large cakes in it at one time." In the old way it required a spider for each cake.

There were no plated knives, but steel, and they

had to be daily scoured with "plenty brickdust on your knife board," but those knives cut like razors. There was no bric-a-brac, few pictures, nothing ornamental in the parlors. One house I remember well had a Bunker Hill monument, made, I guess, of stucco, and stuck all over with gay seashells; it was perhaps 25 or 30 inches high; it made a most commanding appearance on the center-table. When my sister made a tiresomely long call at that house it amused me to try to count the shells.

An old gentleman, called "Old Jimmie Dick" when I remember him, a rich cotton broker (the firm was Dick & Hill), made a voyage to Europe, and brought home some Apollos, and Cupids, and Mercuries, statues in the "altogether," for his parlor. Jimmie Dick was a bachelor, and lived on Canal Street, near Carondelet or Baronne, and had a charming spinster niece keeping house for him, who was so shocked when she saw the figures mounted on pedestals (they were glaring white marble and only a trifle under life size) that she immediately made slips of brown holland and enveloped them, leaving only the heads exposed! I never went to that house but the one time when we surprised her in the act of robing her visitors!

I speak of houses that I visited with my grown sister. It was not *comme il faut* for a young lady to be seen too frequently on the street or to make calls alone. Mother was an invalid and made no visits. Father accompanied sister on ceremonious occasions. I was pressed into service when no one else was available. I feel I am going way back beyond the recollection of my readers, but some of the grandmothers, too old, mayhap, to do their own reading, can recall just such a life, a life that will never be lived again.

VI

A FASHIONABLE FUNCTION IN 1842

IT is hard to realize while we are surrounded by so many housekeeping conveniences what an amount of time, energy, and, above all, knowledge of the craft were necessary to the giving of a reception seventy years ago, when every preparation had to be made in the house and under the watchful supervision of the chatelaine.

There were no chefs to be hired, nor caterers to be summoned, not even a postman to deliver invitations. All that was done "by hand." A darky was sent forth with a basket of nicely "tied up with white ribbons" notes of invitation, and he went from house to house, sending the basket to the occupant, where she not only subtracted her special note, but had the privilege of seeing "who else was invited." And if the darky was bewildered as to his next stopping-place she could enlighten him. This complicated mode of delivering invitations prevailed into the fifties.

The preparations for the supper involved so much

labor that many hosts offered only *eau sucré* or gumbo. There was no cut nor granulated nor pulverized sugar, to be turned from the grocer's bag onto the scales. All sugar except the crude brown, direct from plantations, was in cone-shaped loaves as hard as a stone and weighing several pounds each. These well-wrapped loaves were kept hung (like hams in a smokehouse) from the closet ceiling. They had to be cut into chips by aid of carving knife and hammer, then pounded and rolled until reduced to powder, before that necessary ingredient was ready for use.

There were no fruit extracts, no essences for seasoning, no baking powder to make a half-beaten cake rise, no ground spices, no seedless raisins, no washed (?) currants, no isinglass or gelatine, and to wind up this imperfect list, no egg-beater! Still the thrifty housewife made and served cakes fit for the gods, with only Miss Leslie's cook book to refer to, and that was published in the twenties. Ice cream was seasoned by boiling a whole vanilla bean in the milk; it was frozen in a huge cylinder without any inside fixtures to stir the mixture; it was whirled in the ice tub by hand—and a stout one at that—and required at least one hour, constant labor, to freeze the cream.

For jelly, calves' feet were secured days in

advance, and Madame superintended the making of gelatine. Pink jelly was colored with a drop or two of cochineal, yellow, doctored with lemon, and a beautiful pale green, colored with the strained juice of scalded spinach. These varieties were served in various attractive shapes; and all, even the green, were delicious. These preparations were also complicated by the necessity of procuring all supplies from the early morning market often a mile or more away, and which, besides, closed at 10 o'clock. No stepping to the corner grocery for eggs or butter in an unforeseen emergency, and to the credit of the community the "borrowing habit" was entirely unknown.

I remember a Mrs. Swiler, chiefly because when I went to see her, with an older sister, she "passed around" bananas. Cuban fruits were scarce in those days, and highly prized.

There were no awnings to be used in bad weather; no camp chairs for the invited guests if all came, and all wanted to sit down at the same time; no waterproofs for them to come in; no rubbers to protect feet from rain-soaked sidewalks; no street cars; no public conveyances that people ever hired for such occasions; no private carriages to bump you over rough cobblestones. So, there you are!

Courtyard on Carondelet Street

A FASHIONABLE FUNCTION IN 1842

Arrived after all these tiresome preparations and your own discomfort at my father's house, on Canal Street, to a reception given almost seventy years ago, in honor of Commodore Moore of the Texas navy, who brought to my father letters of introduction from President Mirabeau B. Lamar, of the Republic of Texas, and Gen. Sam Houston of the Texas army!

I have reason to think at this late date, not hearing to the contrary at the time, that the commodore's visit was quite amicable and friendly. If he was escorted by Texas warships! or even arrived in his own flagship! I never knew. With his imposing uniform and a huge gilt star on his breast, a sword at his side, and a rather fierce mustache (mustaches were little worn then), he looked as if he were capable of doing mighty deeds of daring, for the enterprising new republic on our border. He was accompanied by his aide, a callow youth, also in resplendent attire, a sword so long and unwieldy he was continually tripping, and therefore too embarrassingly incommoded to circulate among the ladies. I met that "aide," a real fighter in Texas during the late war. He proudly wore a lone star under the lapel of his coat of Confederate gray, and we had a merry laugh over his naval début. He was Lieut. Fairfax Grey. His sister was the wife of Temple Doswell, and many of her descendants are identified with New Orleans to-day.

Mr. Clay, grand, serene, homely and affable; also Gen. Gaines in his inevitable uniform. The two military and naval officers commanded my admiration, as I sat quietly and unobtrusively in a corner in a way "becoming to a child of nine"—"a chiel amang ye, takin' notes"—but no one took note of the chiel. We had also a jolly itinerant Irish preacher, I think of the Methodist persuasion, whom my father had met at country camp meetings. His call was to travel, and incidentally preach where the harvest was ripe. I remember how, laughingly, he remarked to my father, anent the commodore's visit, that the chief inhabitants of Western Texas were mesquite grass and buffaloes. He was father of John L. Moffitt of Confederate fame, and a very attractive daughter became the wife of President Lamar.

There was dance music—a piano only—but the room was too crowded for more than one attempt at a quadrille. The notabilities, army, navy and State, did not indulge in such frivolity. Life was too serious with them.

These functions generally began at 8 and terminated before the proverbial small hours. So by midnight the last petticoat had fluttered away; and then there followed the clearing up, and, as the old lady said, the "reinstating of affairs," which kept the hostess and her sleepy helpers busy long after the rest of the family had fluttered away also—to the land of Nod.

VII

"When I was young, time had for me the lazy ox's
pace,
But now it's like the blooded horse that means to
win the race."

HERE it is New Year's Day again. It seems
only yesterday when we had such a dull,
stupid New Year's Day. Everybody who
was anybody was out of town, at country mansions
to flourish with the rich, or to old homesteads to
see their folks. Nobody walking the streets, no
shops were open. Those of us who had no rich
friends with country mansions, or no old homesteads
to welcome us, remained gloomily at home, with
shades down, servants off for the day, not even a
basket for cards tied to the doorknob.

Nobody calls now at New Year's. It is out of
fashion, or, rather, the fashion has descended from
parlor to kitchen. When Bridget and Mary don
their finery and repair to Bridget's cousin's to "receive," and Sambo puts on a high shirt collar and
a stovepipe hat, and sallies out on his round of calls,

we have a pick-up dinner, and grandma tries to enliven the family with reminiscences of the New Year's Days of seventy years ago, when her mother and sister "received" in state, and father and brother donned their "stovepipes" and proceeded to fill the society rôle for the year.

In the forties and for years thereafter, New Year's Day was the visiting day for the men, and receiving day for the ladies. All the fathers and grandfathers, in their newest rig, stick in hand, trotted or hobbled around, making the only calls they made from year to year. Before noon, ladies were in their parlors, prinked up, pomatumed up, powdered up, to "receive." Calling began as early as 11, for it was a short winter day, and much to be accomplished. A small stand in the hall held a card receiver, into which a few cards left from last year's stock were placed, so the first caller might not be embarrassed with the fact that he was the first. No one cared to be the very first then, any more than now.

A table of generous dimensions occupied a conspicuous position in the parlor (we never said "drawing room"), with silver tray, an immense and elaborately decorated cake and a grand bowl of foaming eggnog. That was chiefly designed for the beaux. On the dining room sideboard (we did

51

not say "buffet," either) a brandy straight or whisky straight was to be found for those walking-stick ones whose bones were stiff and whose digestion could not brook the fifty different concoctions of eggnog they were liable to find in the fifty different houses. Those varied refreshments, which every caller was expected to at least taste, often worked havoc on the young and spry, to say nothing of the halt and lame.

There were no flower decorations. It was the dead season for plants, and Boston greenhouses were not shipping carloads of roses and carnations to New Orleans in the '40s. Rooms were not darkened, either, to be illuminated with gas or electricity, but windows were thrown wide open to the blessed light of a New Year's Day. Little *cornets* of bonbons and *dragées* were carelessly scattered about. Those cornucopias, very slim and pointed, containing about a spoonful of French confections, were made of stiff, shiny paper, gaudily colored miniatures of impossible French damsels ornamenting them. I have not seen one of those pretty trifles for sixty years. It was quite the style for a swain to send his Dulcinea a *cornet* in the early morning. If the Dulcinea did not happen to receive as many as she wanted, she could buy a few more. One liked to be a Belle!

NEW YEAR'S OF OLD

Living in Canal Street, a little girl was unconsciously taking notes that blossom now in a chronicle of the doings and sayings of those New Year's Days of the early '40s. She enjoyed looking through the open window, onto the broad, unshaded street, watching an endless procession of callers. There were rows of fashionable residences in Canal Street to be visited, and the darting in and out of open doors, as though on earnest business bent, was a sight. The men of that day wore skin-tight pantaloons (we did not call them trousers), often made of light-colored materials. I clearly remember a pea green pair that my brother wore, flickering like a chameleon in and out of open street doors. Those tight-fitting pantaloons were drawn taut over the shoe, a strong leather strap extending under the foot buckled the garment down good and tight, giving the wearer as mincing a gait as the girl in the present-day hobble skirt. The narrow clawhammer coat with tails that hung almost to the knees behind and were scarcely visible in front, had to have the corner of a white handkerchief flutter from the tail pocket.

Military men like Gen. E. P. Gaines (he was in his zenith at that date) and all such who could sport a military record wore stiff stocks about their long necks. Those stocks made the necks ap-

pear abnormally long. They were made of buck-
ram (or sheet iron?), so broad that three straps
were required to buckle them at the back, covered
with black satin, tiny satin bows in front which were
utterly superfluous, for they tied nothing and were
not large enough to be ornamental. The stocks
must have been very trying to the wearers, for they
could not turn their heads when they were buckled
up, and, like the little boy with the broad collar,
could not spit over them. However, they did im-
part a military air of rigidity and stiffness, as though
on dress parade all the time.

I remember Major Waters had a bald spot
on the top of his head and two long strands of
sandy hair on each side which he carefully gathered
up over the bald spot and secured in place by the
aid of a side comb! I used to wish the comb would
fall out, to see what the major would do, for I was
convinced he could not bend his head over that stiff,
formidable stock. The major won his title at the
battle of River Rasin (if you know where that is,
I don't). My father was in the same battle, but
being only seventeen he did not win a title. I don't
suppose that River Rasin engagement amounted to
much anyway, for dear pa did not wear a stock, nor
a military bearing, either. Gen. Persifor Smith was
another stock man who called always at New Year's

and at no other time. And Major Messiah! Dear me, how many of us remember him in the flesh, or can forget the cockaded, epauletted portrait he left behind when he fought his last life's battle?

All the men wore tall silk hats that shone like patent leather. Those hats have not been banished so long ago that all of us have forgotten their monstrosity, still to be seen now and then in old daguerreotypes or *cartes de visite*. They flocked in pairs to do their visiting. It would be a Mardi Gras nowadays to see one of those old-time processions. Men of business, men of prominence, no longer society men, fulfilled their social duty once each year, stepped into the dining room at a nod from mother, who was as rarely in the parlor to "receive," as the men who, at the sideboard, with a flourish of the hand and a cordial toast to the New Year, took a brandy straight. They are long gone. Their sons, the beaux of that day, quietly graduated from the eggnog to the sideboard, become even older men than their fathers, are gone, too.

I remember a very original, entertaining beau of those days saying eggnog was good enough for him, and when he felt he was arriving at the brandy-straight age he meant to kill himself. How would he know when the time for hari-kari came? "When my nose gets spongy." He had a very pronounced

Hebrew nose, by the way. Not so many years ago I heard of him hobbling on crutches. Not only his nose, but his legs were spongy, but he gave no indication that life was not as dear to him as in his salad days.

The younger element, beaux of my grown-up sister, rambled in all day long, hat in hand, with "A happy New Year," a quaff of eggnog, "No cake, thanks," and away like a flash, to go into house after house, do and say the same things, till night would find they had finished their list of calls and eggnog had about finished them. So the great day of the year wore on.

After the house doors were closed at the flirt of the last clawhammer coat tail, cards were counted and comments made as to who had called and who had failed to put in appearance, the wreck of glasses, cake and tray removed, and it was as tired a set of ladies to go to bed as of men to be put into bed.

As the beautiful custom of hospitality spread from the centers of fashion to the outskirts of society the *demi mondaines,* then the small tradesman, then the negroes became infected with the fashion of "receiving" at New Year's, in their various shady abodes. The bon tons gradually relinquished the hospitable and friendly custom of years. Ladies suspended tiny card receivers on the doorknob, and retired behind closed blinds. Those of the old friends of tottering steps and walking sticks, always the last to relinquish a loved habit, wearily dropped cards into the little basket and passed on to the next closed door. Now the anniversary, instead of being one of pleasant greetings, is as stupid and dull as any day in the calendar, unless, as I have said, one has a friend with a "cottage by the sea" or a château on the hilltop and is also endowed with the spirit of hospitality to ask one to spend the week-end and take an eggnog or a brandy straight.

VIII

THE shopping region of New Orleans was confined to Chartres and Royal Streets seventy years ago. It was late in the fifties when the first movement was made to more commodious and less crowded locations on Canal Street, and Olympe, the fashionable modiste, was the venturesome pioneer.

Woodlief's was the leading store on Chartres Street and Barrière's on Royal, where could be found all the French *nouveautés* of the day, beautiful *barèges,* Marcelines and chiné silks, organdies stamped in gorgeous designs, to be made up with wreathed and bouquet flounces, but, above and beyond all for utility and beauty, were the imported French calicoes, fine texture, fast colors. It was before the day of aniline and diamond dyes; blues were indigo, reds were cochineal pure and unadulterated; so those lovely goods, printed in rich designs—often the graceful palm-leaf pattern—could be "made over," turned upside down and hindpart before, indefinitely, for they never wore out or lost color, and were cheap at fifty cents a yard. None but those in mourning wore black; even the men wore blue or bottle green coats, gay flowered vests and tan-colored pantaloons. I call to mind one ultra-fashionable beau who delighted in a pair of sage green "pants."

The ladies' toilets were still more gay; even the elderly ones wore bright colors. The first black silk dress worn on the street, and that was in '49, was proudly displayed by Miss Mathilde Eustis, who had relatives in France who kept her *en rapport* with the latest Parisian style. Hers was a soft Marceline silk; even the name, much less the article, is as extinct as the *barège* and *crêpe lisse* of those far away days. It was at Woodlief's or Bar-rières these goods were displayed on shelves and counters. There were no show windows, no dressed and draped wax figures to tempt the passerby.

Mme. Pluche's shop, on the corner of Royal and Conti, had one window where a few trifles were occasionally displayed on the sill or hung, carefully draped on the side, so as not to intercept the light. Madame was all French and dealt only in French importations. Mme. Frey was on Chartres Street. Her specialty (all had specialties; there was no shop

59

room for a miscellaneous stock of goods) was *mantillas, visites, cardinals* and other confections to envelop the graceful mesdames *en flânant.* I call to mind a *visite* of thinnest muslin, heavily embroidered (no Hamburg or machine embroidery in those days), lined with blue silk, blue cords and tassels for a finish. It was worn by a belle of the forties, and Mme. Frey claimed to have imported it. The madame was not French. She had a figure no French woman would have submitted to, a fog-horn voice and a well-defined mustache, but her taste was the best and her dictum in her specialty was final.

The fashionable milliner was Olympe. Her specialty was imported *chapeaux.* She did not—ostensibly, at least—make or even trim *chapeaux.* Olympe's ways were persuasive beyond resistance. She met her customer at the door with "Ah, madame"—she had brought from Paris the very bonnet for you! No one had seen it; it was yours! And Mam'zelle Adèle was told to bring Mme. X's *chapeau.* It fit to a *merveille!* It was an inspiration! And so Mme. X had her special bonnet sent home in a fancy box by the hand of a dainty *grisette.* Olympe was the first of her class to make a specialty of delivering the goods. And Monsieur X, though he may have called her "Old Imp," paid the bill with all the extras of specialty and delivery included, though not itemized. Those were bonnets to shade the face—a light blue satin shirred lengthwise; *crêpe lisse,* same color, shirred crosswise over it, forming indistinct blocks; and a *tout aller,* of raspberry silk, shirred "every which way," are two that I recall.

Madame a-shopping went followed by a servant to bring home the packages. Gloves, one button only, were light colored, pink, lavender, lemon, rarely white; and for ordinary wear bottle green gloves were considered very *comme il faut.* They harmonized with the green *barège* veil that every lady had for shopping.

Our shopping trip would be incomplete if we failed to call on an old Scotch couple who had a lace store under Col. Winthrop's residence on Royal Street. The store had a door and a window, and the nice old parties who had such a prodigious Scotch brogue one would scarcely understand them, could, by a little skill, entertain three customers at one and the same time. If one extra shopper appeared, Mr. Syme disappeared, leaving the old lady to attend to business. She was almost blind from cataract, a canny old soul and not anyways blind to business advantages. I am pleased to add they retired after a few busy years quite well-to-do. There was Seibricht, on Royal Street, a furniture dealer, and still further down Royal Seignoret, in the same lucrative business, for I do not recall they had any competitors. Memory does not go beyond the time when Hyde and Goodrich were not the jewelers; and Loveille, on the corner of Customhouse and Royal, the grocer, for all foreign wines, cheeses, etc. Never do I see such Parmesan as we got from Loveille in my early days.

William McKean had a bookshop on Camp Street, a few doors above Canal. Billy McKean, as the irreverent called him, was a picture of Pickwick, and a clever, kindly old man was he. There was a round table in the rear of his shop, where one found a comfortable chair and a few books to browse over. In my childhood I was always a welcome visitor to that round table, for I always "sat quiet and just read," as dear old Mr. McKean told me. As I turn the pages of my book of memories not only the names but the very faces of these shopkeepers of seventy years ago come to me, all smiles and winning ways, and way back I fly to my pantalette and pigtail days, so happy in these dreams that will never be reality to any place or people.

There were no restaurants, no lunch counters, no tea rooms, and (bless their dear hearts, who started it!) no woman's exchange, no place in the whole city where a lady could drop in, after all this round of shopping, take a comfortable seat and order even a sandwich, or any kind of refreshment. One could take an éclair at Vincent's, corner of Royal and Orleans, but éclairs have no satisfying quality.

There was a large hotel (there may be still—it is sixty years since I saw it), mostly consisting of spacious verandas, up and down and all around, at the lake end of the shellroad, where parties could have a fish dinner and enjoy the salt breezes, but a dinner at "Lake End" was an occasion, not a climax to a shopping trip. The old shellroad was a long drive, Bayou St. John on one side, swamps on the other, green with rushes and palmetto, clothed with gay flowers of the swamp flag. The road terminated at Lake Pontchartrain, and there the restful piazza and well-served dinner refreshed the inner woman.

I am speaking of the gentler sex. No doubt there were myriads of cabarets and eating places for men on pleasure or business bent. Three o'clock was the universal dinner hour, so the discreet *mesdames* were able to return to the city and be ready by early candlelight for the inevitable "hand round" tea.

Then there was Carrollton Garden (I think it is dead and buried now). There was a short railroad leading to Carrollton; one could see open fields and grazing cattle from the car windows as one crept along. Except a still shorter railroad to the Lake, connecting with the Lake boats, I think the rural road to Carrollton was the only one leading out of the city. The Carrollton hotel, like the Lake one, was all verandas. I never knew of any guest staying there, even one night, but there was a dear little garden and lots of summer houses and pagodas, covered with jasmines and honeysuckle vines. One could get lemonade or orgeat or orange flower syrup, and return to the city with a great bouquet of monthly roses, to show one had been on an excursion. A great monthly rose hedge, true to its name, always in bloom, surrounded the premises. To see a monthly rose now is to see old Carrollton gardens in the forties.

1/6/2011 4:25 PM   **Sales Receipt #34379**
Store: 1

Friends of the Cabildo
523 St Ann Street
New Orleans, LA 70116
504-524-9118
www.friendsofthecabildo.org

Cashier: James

Item #	Qty	Price	Ext Price
166	1	$19.95	$19.95 T
Social Life Old N.O.1			

	Subtotal:	$19.95
Local Sales Tax	9 % Tax:	+ $1.80
RECEIPT TOTAL:		**$21.75**

Amount Tendered: $22.00
Change Given: $0.25

Cash: $22.00

Thanks for shopping with us!

34379

IX

THE OLD FRENCH OPERA HOUSE

IT was on Orleans Street, near Royal—I don't have to "shut my eyes and think very hard," as the Marchioness said to Dick Swiveller, to see the old Opera House and all the dear people in it, and hear its entrancing music. We had "Norma" and "Lucia di Lammermoor" and "Robert le Diable" and "La Dame Blanche," "Huguenots," "Le Prophête," just those dear old melodious operas, the music so thrillingly catchy that half the young men hummed or whistled snatches of it on their way home.

There were no single seats for ladies, only four-seated boxes. The pit, to all appearances, was for elderly, bald gentlemen only, for the beaux, the fashionable eligibles, wandered around in the intermissions or "stood at attention" in the narrow lobbies behind the boxes during the performances. Except the two stage boxes, which were more ample, and also afforded sly glimpses towards the wings and flies, all were planned for four occupants. Also, all were subscribed for by the season. There was also a row of latticed boxes in the rear of the dress circle, usually occupied by persons in mourning, or the dear old *messieurs et mesdames,* who were not chaperoning a *mademoiselle.* One stage box belonged, by right of long-continued possession, to Mr.

THE OLD FRENCH OPERA HOUSE.

and Mrs. Cuthbert Bullitt. The opposite box was *la loge des lions,* and no less than a dozen lions wandered in and out of it during an evening. Some were blasé and looked dreadfully bored, a few were young and frisky, but every mortal one of them possessed a pompous and self-important mien.

If weather permitted (we had to consider the

weather, as everybody walked) and the opera a favorite, every seat would be occupied at 8 o'clock, and everybody quiet to enjoy the very first notes of the overture. All the fashionable young folks, even if they could not play or whistle "Yankee Doodle," felt the opera was absolutely necessary to their social success and happiness. The box was only five dollars a night, and pater-familias certainly could afford that!

Think of five dollars for four seats at the most fashionable Opera House in the land then, and compare it with five dollars for one seat in the topmost gallery of the most fashionable house in the land to-day. Can one wonder we old people who sit by our fire and pay the bills wag our heads and talk of the degenerate times?

Toilets in our day were simple, too. French muslins trimmed with real lace, pink and blue *barèges* with ribbons. Who sees a *barège* now? No need of jeweled stomachers, ropes of priceless pearls or diamond tiaras to embellish those Creole ladies, many of whom were direct descendants of French nobles; not a few could claim a drop of even royal blood.

Who were the beaux? And where are they now? If any are living they are too old to hobble into the pit and sit beside the old, bald men.

It was quite the vogue to saunter into Vincent's, at the corner, on the way home. Vincent's was a great place and he treated his customers with so much "confidence." One could browse about the glass cases of pâtés, *brioches,* éclairs, méringues, and all such toothsome delicacies, peck at this and peck at that, lay a dime on the counter and walk out. A large Broadway firm in New York attempted that way of conducting a lunch counter and had such a tremendous patronage that it promptly failed. Men went for breakfast and shopping parties for lunch, instead of dropping in *en passant* for an éclair.

As I said, we walked. There were no street cars, no 'buses and precious few people had carriages to ride in. So we gaily walked from Vincent's to our respective homes, where a cup of hot coffee put us in condition for bed and slumber.

Monday morning Mme. Casimir or Mam'zelle Victorine comes to sew all day like wild for seventy-five cents, and tells how splendidly Rosa de Vries (the prima donna) sang *"Robert, toi que j'aime"* last night. She always goes, *"Oui, madame, toujours,"* to the opera Sunday. Later, dusky Henriette Blondéau comes, with her *tignon* stuck full of pins and the deep pockets of her apron bulging with sticks of bandoline, pots of pomade, hairpins and a bandeau comb, to dress the hair of mademoiselle. She also had to tell how fine was "Robert," but she prefers De Vries in "Norma," "*moi*." The Casimirs lived in a kind of cubby-hole way down Ste. Anne Street. M. Casimir was assistant in a barber shop near the French Market, but such were the gallery gods Sunday nights, and no mean critics were they. Our nights were Tuesday and Saturday.

Society loves a bit of gossip, and we had a delightful dish of it about this time, furnished us by a denizen of Canal Street. He was "horribly English, you know." As French was the fashion then, it was an impertinence to swagger with English airs. The John Bull in question, with his wife all decked out in her Sunday war paint and feathers, found a woman calmly seated in his pew at Christ Church, a plainly dressed, common appearing woman, who didn't even have a flower in her bonnet. The pew door was opened wide and a gesture accompanied it, which the common-looking somebody did not fail to comprehend. She promptly rose and retired into the aisle; a seat was offered her nearer the door of the church, which she graciously accepted. Lady Mary Wortley Montagu had asked for a seat in that pew, as she bore a letter of introduction to its occupant. This incident gave us great merriment, for the inhospitable Englishman had been boasting of the coming of Lady Mary. I introduce it here, for it has a moral which gives a Sunday school flavor to my opera reminiscences. Now they have all gone where they are happily singing, I hope, even better than Rosa de Vries, and where there are no doors to the pews.

X

MURAL DECORATIONS AND PORTRAITS OF THE PAST

THE pendulum is swinging. Landscape wall papers, after a seventy years' truce, are on the warpath, to vanquish damask hangings and other fabrics that are traps for moths and dust and microbes, we old-time people aver. Now, in view of the return to favor of landscape wall papers, some elegant, expensive and striking specimens rise in my memory, and clamor to be once more displayed to the public.

I vividly remember a decorated wall at a school under the charge of a superannuated Episcopal clergyman. His aged wife must have possessed considerable artistic ability, for she painted, on the parlor walls, mythological subjects, as befits a school teacher's, if not a preacher's, residence. There were Diana and her nymphs (quite modestly wrapped in floating draperies) on one side the room, and opposite, was Aurora in her chariot, driving her team of doves. They were up in the dawning sky, and below was such greenery as I presume old Mrs. Ward thought belonged to the period of gods and goddesses, but it was strangely like the bushes and trees in her own back yard. Various other figures were floating or languishing about. The colors, on the whole, were not brilliant; in fact, artistically subdued. That bit of mural adornment was a curiosity to all. I, a little child, thought it most wonderful, and it was. All these landscape walls had a three or four-foot base of a solid color, surmounted by a band of wood, called in those days "chair boarding." So the figures came near the level of the eye.

Years after the two old people had joined the immortals, I had occasion to call at the house. It was a great disappointment to find the parlor wall covered with stiff paper, representing slabs of white marble (marble, of all things, in that dingy red-brick house!). Aurora and Diana, and perhaps Calypso, for I imagine the scope was sufficiently extensive to comprise such a picturesque immortal, were buried under simulated marble. A weather-beaten portrait of Major Morgan in full uniform hung right over the spot where Aurora drove her fluttering birds. I looked at the desecration in dismay, when the voice of old black mammy was heard. "Dat is Mars Major in his rag-gi-ments; you never know'd him?" No, I didn't. "And dat odder portrait over dar" (pointing to a simpering girl with curly hair) "is Miss Merriky 'fore she married de major." Where are those old portraits now? The whirligig of time has doubtless whirled them away to some obscure closet or garret, where, with faces turned to the wall, they await a time when there will be a general cleaning up or tearing down—then where? *Sic transit!*

TYPICAL OLD NEW ORLEANS DWELLING.

I recall, in later life, a wonderful wall paper on the broad hall of Judge Chinn's house in West Baton Rouge. That was very gay and brilliant, somewhat after the Watteau style, swains playing on impossible instruments to beauties in various listening attitudes; lambs gamboling in the distance, birds flying about amid lovely foliage, horsemen on galloping steeds with extraordinary trappings. How I did love that wall! It was never permitted the family to cover all that glory with "pillars and panels," for the house, shortly after my visit, was destroyed by fire, and the debonair ladies, prancing steeds and all went up in one great holocaust.

The new house that rose over the ashes was aptly called Whitehall. It was all white, inside and out, broad, dead white walls, grand balconies all around the mansion dead white; white steps led to the lawn, and the trees surrounding had their trunks whitewashed as high as could be reached by a long pole and a brush. All the old portraits and some awful prints (it was long before the chromo era) were fished out of closets and other hiding places and hung about on the white walls. One old man with a tremendously long neck and a stiff black stock to help hold up his head, and a fierce look, had a pair of eyes that looked like great daubs of ink. His portrait decorated the parlor. I was warned not to handle the gilt-edged books and little trinkets on the marble-top center-table, "for your Cousin Christopher will see you; notice, whichever way you turn his eyes will follow you." I was mortally afraid of that old spook till little black Comfort told me, "Laws! if dem eyes could hurt we'd all be'n daid in dis house."

At "The Oaks," Dr. Patrick's plantation, the wall paper illustrated scenes from China, in colors not gorgeous, like the last mentioned, neither was the house so pretentious. There was no broad, high ceilinged hall to ornament with startling figures that seemed to jump at you. The orderly processions of pigtailed Chinamen in sepia tints could not by any possibility get on one's nerves. Whole processions wended their way to impossible temples, wedding processions, palanquins, and all that; funeral processions dwindled away to a mere point in the distance, all becomingly solemn, until some of the irrepressible Patrick children, with black pencil, or charcoal, or ink, put pipes into all the mouths and clouds of smoke therefrom spotted the landscape. Moral suasion was the discipline of the Patrick children, so that freak was not probably followed by afterclaps, but the Chinese were promptly marched off, and the inevitable white walls were the result.

Family portraits came forth to brighten the room. One notable one that superseded the Chinese wall paper was a full-length portrait of Gov. Poindexter's (everybody knows "Old Poins" was the first Governor of the State of Mississippi) first wife, who was a sister of Mrs. Patrick. She was a vision of beauty, in full evening dress. Facing her was the glum, "sandy complected" Governor, not one bit fascinated by the sight of his wife's smiling face.

The fashionable portrait painter of the time was

75

Moïse; it was he who painted the author's portrait shortly after her marriage. He was a dashing, improvident genius, and many of his portraits were executed to cancel debts. At one time he designed and had made for my husband, in settlement for a loan, a handsome silver lidded bowl with alcohol lamp beneath. It was known as a *pousse café* and was used to serve hot punch to after-dinner parties. I am glad to say it has survived all the family vicissitudes, and is an honored heirloom, in company with a *repoussé* silver pitcher, which we won as a prize for cattle at the Louisiana State Fair, described in a later chapter.

At John C. Miller's place the house was only one story, but it spread over what seemed to be a half acre of land. A square hall, which was a favorite lounging place for everybody, had wall paper delineating scenes from India. Women walked toward the Ganges river, smilingly tripping along with huge water jars on their shoulders, in full view of another woman descending the steps of a temple, with a naked baby, poised aloft, to be thrown into the sacred Ganges. A crocodile ruffled the blue (very blue) waters, with jaws distended, ready to complete the sacrifice. That sacred river seemed to course all around the hall, for on another side were a number of bathers, who appeared to be utterly

MURAL DECORATIONS AND PORTRAITS

oblivious of their vicinity to the mother and babe, not to mention the awful crocodile.

The culmination of landscape wall paper must have been reached in the Minor plantation dwelling in Ascension parish. Mrs. Minor had received this plantation as a legacy, and she was so loyal to the donor that the entreaties of her children to "cover that wall" did not prevail. It was after that style of mural decoration was of the past, that I visited the Minors. The hall was broad and long, adorned with real jungle scenes from India. A great tiger jumped out of dense thickets toward savages, who were fleeing in terror. Tall trees reached to the ceiling, with gaudily striped boa constrictors wound around their trunks; hissing snakes peered out of jungles; birds of gay plumage, paroquets, parrots, peacocks everywhere, some way up, almost out of sight in the greenery; monkeys swung from limb to limb; ourang-outangs, and lots of almost naked, dark-skinned natives wandered about. To cap the climax, right close to the steps one had to mount to the story above was a lair of ferocious lions!

I spent hours studying that astonishing wall paper, and I applauded Mrs. Minor's decision, "The old man put it there; it shall stay; he liked it, so do I." It was in 1849 I made that never-to-be-forgot-

77

ten trip to jungle land. The house may still be there; I don't know; but I warrant that decorated hall has been "done over," especially if little children ever came to invade the premises. Upon the departure of landscape wall paper, the pendulum swung to depressing simplicity of dead white walls or else "pillared and paneled," which is scarcely one degree better.

Old portraits and any kind of inartistic picture or print were brought forth to gratify the eye unaccustomed to such monotony. Only a few years ago I asked: "What became of that military epauletted portrait of old Major Messiah that always hung in your mother's hall when we were children?" "Oh, it was hanging twenty or more years ago in the office of a hardware concern down town. Don't know where it is now."

After the war, inquiring for a lot of portraits of various degrees of merit and demerit that disappeared when the Yankees left, we heard that some were in negro cabins in West Feliciana. So they come and are appreciated, those images of loved ones. So they often go, and are despised by those who follow us, and who, perchance, never knew the original. Now the questions arise, will landscape wall papers really return? And in their pristine splendor? Surely the scope in brilliancy and variety

could not be excelled. The limit was reached almost seventy years ago, and naturally (I was a
child then) comes as vividly to my mind as the counterfeit face of my ancestor with eyes following me
all around the room. The tigers and ourang-
outangs, even the den of lions and the crocodile of
the Ganges, never made my little soul quake like the
searching eyes of "my Cousin Christopher."

XI

THOUGHTS OF OLD

I SHALL begin to think I am in my second childhood by and by. I have just been reading
of a fashionable wedding where the bride and
her attendants carried flat bouquets with lace paper
frills. I don't doubt the revival of the *porte bouquet* will come next, the slender bouquet holders
made of filigree silver with a dagger like a short
hatpin to stick clear through and secure the bouquet—a chain and ring attached to the holder and
all could be hung from the finger. I used to think,
a childish looker-on, that it was pretty to see the
ladies in a quadrille "balancing to your partners,"
"ladies changing," etc., each with a tight little bouquet in a trim little holder swinging and banging
about from the chain.

Later the *porte bouquets* were abandoned, but
the stiff little posies, in their lacy frills, remained.
They were symmetrical, a camellia japonica, surrounded by a tiny row of heliotrope, then a row of
Grand Duke jasmine, one of violets, finally a *soup-
çon* of greenery, and the paper bed. James Pollock

had a fund of such rare flowers to draw from, for though the Pollock home down on Royal street was the simplest of old Creole houses, flush on the street,

A CREOLE PARTERRE.

only two steps from the *banquette* leading into a modest parlor, there was a tiny *parterre* in the rear, a vision of the most choice collection of plants. How it was managed and cultivated I don't know, for it was hemmed in on all sides by buildings that intercepted much of the air and almost all of the sun's rays. Still those camellias, Grand Dukes and violets thrived and bloomed, and delighted the heart of any girl to whom James, the best dancer in society, sent them in one of those tight little bouquets on the eve of a dance.

81

I have to-day a much larger *parterre* in my back-yard, open to sun and rain and wind, but no amount of coddling brings anything better than dock-weed and tie-grass. I leave it to the climate of my own sunny Southland to explain the problem. The *porte bouquet* will no doubt come in time. I for one will hail an old friend, if I am "on deck" when it arrives.

Last Christmas what should my granddaughter receive but a mob cap of gold lace! almost exactly like one my mother wore before I can remember. Caps! Every woman when she arrived at middle age, and some who found them becoming at an earlier age, wore caps. My mother was considered very tasty and expert at cap-trimming. She had a papier maché, or soft wood dummy head—I know she stuck pins into it—on which she fashioned her caps.

Mechlin lace (one rarely sees it now) was considered the fashionable cap lace. Remember cotton laces and Italian laces and machine-made laces were not in existence in those days, neither were Hamburg embroideries and Nottingham curtains, two awful products of to-day; and a thousand other make-believes, cheap and tawdry now. When mother's fine Mechlin edgings became soiled she "did them up" herself, clapping the damp lace in her hands, pulling out and straightening the delicate edges—drying them without heat; and she had a deft way, too, of what she called "pinching" with her dainty fingers; she knife pleated it. The net foundation was fitted to the wooden head, the lace was attached in folds and frills, and little pink rosebuds or some other tiny flower scattered tastefully here and there. Behold a dress cap! One can imagine the care and taste and time and thought consumed in its manufacture. And how the old lady must have appeared when in full dress!

Many of those dames wore little bunches of black curls to enhance the effect, those tight, stiff little curls that looked like they had been wound on a slate-pencil. Dear Mrs. Leonard Matthews always wore the black curls. Even a few years after the war I met the sweet old lady, curls and all, jet black, tight little curls, and she looked scarcely older than in my earliest recollection of her.

Well, I must return to cap trimmings to tell of a bride. She must have been in the neighborhood of seventy, for she made what her friends called a suitable match with a widower long past that age. They came to the St. Charles Hotel on a kind of honeymoon trip. She decorated her head, oh, ye cherubim and seraphim! with a fussy cap sprinkled with sprays of orange flowers!

I, who revel in a towering white pompadour,

have just had the present of a soft silk cap, with frills and bows. I presume it will be useful on the breezy piazzas of the mountains a week hence; but it looks to me now that the caps of our mothers and grandmothers are on the march hitherward. I possess a few "Moniteurs des Dames," dated in the late forties, that contain pictures and patterns for "bonnets," as they were called. Who knows but they may be useful yet?

Now, "in regard to" (as a lady we all know prefaces every remark)—"in regard to" frills, in my young days we had to make our own frills. Nobody had dreamed even of machine-made ruchings any more than of vehicles that run all over the streets without the aid of horses. We made our frills of lawn, neatly gathered on to a band, and what is more, they had to be fluted with hot irons. The making was not beyond everybody's skill, but the "doing up" and fluting was way beyond me, as beyond many others. How queer it is, when we recall to mind the images of people so long absent that they are almost forgotten, the image presents itself, emphasized by some peculiarity of dress or speech. When I think of Dr. Bein's daughter Susanna, whom I knew and loved so well, it is with the beautifully fluted frill she always wore and so excited my envy. Now, every Biddy in the kitchen and every little darky one sees wandering around wears handsomer frills than Susanna and I ever dreamed of.

Parasols had heavy fringes; so, to show to advantage, they were carried upside down, the ferule end fitted with a ring to be, like the bouquet holders, hung from the finger. My sister had a blue parasol, with pink fringe, that I thought too beautiful for words. How I should laugh at it now!

Best frocks, such as could be utilized for dinners and parties, were made with short sleeves, "caps," they were called, and tapes sewed in the armholes; long sleeves similarly equipped were tied in under the "caps." I used to see even party guests take off their sleeves as they put on their gloves to descend to the dancing room. Black, heelless slippers, with narrow black ribbons, wound over the instep, and crossed and recrossed from ankle, way up, over white stockings, were the style; it was a pretty fashion.

I recall the autumn of 1849, when I, a young girl, was at the Astor House, in New York. Coming downstairs one morning to breakfast, how surprised I was at glaring notices posted on walls and doors, "Hop to-night." You may well believe I was at the hop, though I had no suitable dress. I was only a looker-on.

When I mentioned slippers I recalled that hotel hop, for Mme. Le Vert wore a pink silk dress and pink satin slippers, all laced up and tied up with broad pink ribbons. Nobody had ever seen the like before. Mme. Walton, her mother, was on hand, and hopped, too, just as spry a hop as any young girl. I contrived to sidle along and keep near to Mme. Le Vert, for I was as fascinated as any one of her numerous beaux. Dr. Le Vert, by the way, had just started on a trip to Europe for his health. Going to Europe then was like taking a trip to Mars now.

I heard Mme. Le Vert talking to four different swains in four different languages. I believe she considered her linguistic versatility her strong point. She surely was a most remarkable woman. She was as tender and sweet to me, a very plain, simple, unattractive girl, as to her swellest friends. One does not easily forget such an episode of early life. I never met Mme. Le Vert after that autumn. We all returned South together on the Crescent City, the pioneer steamer between New York and New Orleans.

I will not moralize or sermonize over these reminiscences. They are all of the dead past. Both fashions and people are gone.

XII

WEDDING CUSTOMS THEN AND NOW

WE were lingering about the breakfast table having such a comfortable, chatty review of the last night's party, when a familiar voice was heard. "Oh! congratulate me; we have captured him; they are engaged." That was the first time I had ever heard an "announcement" from headquarters. It was made to Mrs. Slocomb, in her library. There followed many amusing particulars, audible to us, in the adjoining room, but we were discreet young girls; perhaps that was one reason we were among the very few invited to the wedding, which so quickly followed the engagement that it was a complete surprise to the whole community.

Sixty years ago only Catholics went to the sanctuary for a wedding ceremony. Protestant weddings were home affairs, necessarily confined to family and nearest friends. Houses being limited in space, company was limited in number. No city house could boast of a ballroom; few had "double parlors."

At the wedding whose "announcement" was such a surprise to us, I think our family and the Slo-combs were the only guests, except the families of the groom's business associates. The idea of having a grand reception to announce a marriage engage-ment, to which everybody who is anybody is invited, was unheard of. The anxiety, too, of the parties interested to get the news in a suitable form in the daily papers, for the butcher boy and the sewing girl, out of the social swim, to read, accompanied by the genealogies of the engaged people, the wealth of the girl and how she came by it, and the numbers of clubs of which the young man is a mem-ber, as though the money and the clubs were "the chief end of man," was unheard of, too. We did things on a very different scale sixty years ago!

I recall my astonishment when Elèna Longer told me her sister Héda was married the night before, for Elèna and I (we were ten years old at the time) had played together all that day of the wedding, and not a hint was imparted to me of the impending event. I had not even heard the name of Mr. Charles Kock, the fiancé, mentioned. There were already six married daughters, with hosts of chil-dren, at that time in the Longer family, so there could have been little room on such an occasion for outsiders, even if their presence had been desired.

Wedding presents were not made, either. The first time we saw a display of wedding gifts, how surprised we were, and how we wondered as to how it happened! There were not many, nor were they expensive, so for ever so long I could have given the list and the names of the donors. Dear Maria Shute, who, as I remember, was the bridesmaid, presented a pearl-handled paper cutter! That article might have escaped my memory, along with the others, but years after that wedding I met Maria, then Mrs. Babcock, and we talked of it all, and had a merry laugh over the paper cutter.

Fifty-eight years ago, when I married, I was surprised by a solitary wedding present, a napkin ring! From the most unexpected source it came. The giver is long since dead and gone; dead and gone also is the napkin ring.

At the wedding of Caroline Hennen to Mr. Muir, the first I ever attended, there were not a dozen guests, but the rooms were filled, indeed the Hennen family easily filled one of them. At this wedding we met Mr. William Babcock from New York, a forty-niner en route to California (this was in 1849). The following day I went with him to call on and introduce him to his young cousin, an intimate friend of mine he was desirous of meeting. She was of that handsome family of Smiths, a niece of Mrs. Labouisse. I never saw either him or her afterwards, for within the following fortnight they quietly married and started "round the Horn" to San Francisco. More than fifty years after I saw their children and grandchildren in California.

Some of us must remember genial, gossipy Mrs. Garnet Duncant, the *bon vivant,* so bright, so fat and so entertaining? She it was who called one day (sixty years ago) to tell us Amelia Zacharie had married her invalid cousin, and sailed away with him. Those two are the only cases I recall of wedding trips, and both were permanent trips, for there was no intention of a return to New Orleans of either couple. It was the fashion for the newly-mated to remain quietly in the home nest, until one of their very own be made ready for their reception.

James Pollock, I recall to mind, made a late appearance (in 1850) at a dance given by the Lanfears, on Julia street, that old "13 Buildings." The Lanfears were the last to leave that once fashionable row. Pollock swept in late, full of apologies. His sister Mana had married that evening and he was detained.

The only other wedding trip I can chronicle was one where the bridegroom went alone. Do you remember what an excitement there was, years ago, when a wealthy young man disappeared from the side of his bride the morning after the wedding? There were no wires or wireless then to facilitate the hunt, undertaken with frantic haste, and continuing two mortally anxious weeks. He was eventually discovered, in a semi-conscious, dazed condition, on a wharfboat at Baton Rouge, or some such river town. He recovered from that attack, to be blown away by another "brain storm" a few years later. It was twenty years after this second disappearance that the courts pronounced him dead, and the widow permitted to administer on the estate.

In those days old maids were rare. Every girl, so to say, married. The few exceptions served to emphasize the rarity of an unmated female.

Divorces were so rare when I was young that they were practically unknown in polite circles. I know of cases, and you would know of them, too, if I mentioned names, where men sent their erring or cast-off wives, not to Coventry, but to Paris, and made them stay there. One such died in Paris lately at the age of ninety-five, who was packed off, under a cloud of suspicion. There was no divorce, no open scandal. She simply went and stayed! He simply stayed!

Last winter I was invited to a view (sounds like a picture exhibit!) of the trousseau and wedding gifts of a fashionable young lady. I was stunnned

with amazement! A large room filled to overflow-
ing with glass, china, silver, mirrors, everything a
body could require, and a vast array of utterly useless articles! and the trousseau which the tired
mother, who has had nervous prostration ever since,
spent months accumulating in Paris. My gracious!
the best *blanchisseuse* in the land could not cope successfully with all that flimsy finery, laces and ribbons. I could only look and wonder, "What can
all this lead to?" (I add here, anticipating events:
It led to an apartment and one maid servant.)
The young man was a salaried clerk, and the young
girl utterly unfit to care for even the superabun-
dance of china and silver, so much more than they
could possibly find use for in a three-story house,
not to mention a six-room apartment and "light
housekeeping." I wonder if the whirligig of time
won't bring back some of the simplicity of my day?

Already it is the style to "fire out of sight" the
useless bric-a-brac ornaments that twenty years ago
cluttered up drawing rooms till one had to pick her
way carefully lest she stumble over a blue china cat,
or tilt over a bandy-leg table covered with ivory
idols and Chinese mandarins with bobbing heads.
Some of the most fashionable drawing rooms to-day
are already so stripped of furniture one has to wander around quite a bit to find a chair to sit on; not

even a pier mirror to prink before, nor a parlor clock, flanked by "side pieces," on the mantel. All that banished for stunning simplicity. Not so, however, the costumes and entertainments, which are becoming, so it seems to a near-sighted old lady, more and more luxurious. Perhaps this extreme (we all dote on extremes) of simplicity will come to take the place of many other equally absurd extremes of the present day. *Qui vivra verra.*

XIII

A COUNTRY WEDDING IN 1846

WE missed the train! and here we were in the old Bayou Sara Hotel, looking for some kind of locomotion. We had eighteen miles to make, and if the *Belle Creole* had made the run we would have been all right, but the *Belle Creole* was not a flier; it had no time for arrivals or departures; it just jogged along at its own good will, answering every call, running all sorts of antics up and down the river. Dick started out to see what he could do.

I sat on the dirty porch, looking through November china trees towards the river. Is there anything more depressing than a view of china trees in November? The pretty, fragrant, blue flowers long gone, and the mocking birds (nobody ever heard of English sparrows then!) that had drunk their fill of intoxicating liquor from the scattering china berries were gone too. The train we had missed, the dear old *Belle Creole* always missed, was a kind of private affair. The whole outfit, about twenty miles of track, the lumbering cars, the antiquated engines, and I think, too, the scattering woods that supplied the fuel were all the private property of the McGehees. The McGehees had a cotton factory in the neighborhood of Woodville, twenty miles from the river. They had one train, cheap and dirty, that made one trip a day, going with freight very early in the morning, returning later, with freight and one small passenger car for the owner's use. This concern stopped for wood and water and nothing else, and was the only means of transport for "casuals" like ourselves from the river to Woodville. Ladies going back and forth and gentlemen of leisure used their own conveyance, a turtle-back affair that was entered by a row of steps. The dear *Belle Creole* was too much of a convenience to have a time table, so it was useless to construct a time table and plan to "connect" with that equally free and easy train. Some disgruntled chap chalked on an unused car, left on the rails as a depot, "We belong to the McGehees, and go when we please."

Well, to make the matter short, though it was long to me, on that dirty porch by the china trees, Dick found a man with a turtle-top coach, and a harness mended by cords and stakes and bits of rawhide. The man had a mended look, too, but he

95

was sober, and for a good, round sum agreed to take us to Laurel Hill. Laurel Hill, where we proposed to go, was a post office station, about ten miles from Woodville and four miles across country. We meandered along, tired and out of all patience. At the date of this tramp I was a little girl and not given to moralizing. When we arrived at Laurel Hill we were told, "Creek is up; been a big rain somewhere; not even a horseman has crossed all day." There was no accommodation for man or beast at the queer little depot, no place to sit and nothing to sit on. It was long after dark, and there was no one to tell us the story of the high water but a negro man, who was shutting up the one door of the building. There was nothing left us but to go to the nearest plantation house and ask for lodgings.

I was so tired I felt we had gone ten miles further when we reached Major Dick Haile's, though it really was only a few miles. The tired horses and the sleepy driver made slow work. There was a gate and an opening, but the house was pitch dark, every door closed and everybody apparently asleep. The nags were willing to stand, unhitched, beside the fence; not an automobile or flying machine could have scared them; they were asleep, too.

After much knocking and calling at what seemed

to be the door of entrance, an old gentleman, candle in hand and very scantily dressed, demanded to know what was wanted. My brother called that we were on our way to the General's, and we could not cross the creek, so we begged the privilege of a lodging for the night.

"General's for the wedding? Come right in." A brighter light was procured, and before we were seated in the reception room we heard the hospitable voice, "Put your carriage under the shed, give those horses a good feed, then come to the kitchen and get a bite for yourself." The two young daughters came in, hurriedly dressed (people did not have bathrobes and wrappers seventy years ago). I was awfully tired and awfully sleepy, and I began to think our lodgings were to be parlor chairs, long before the dining room door was opened, and the genial old gentleman, in night shirt and trousers, led the way to the table. We had fried chicken, hot cornbread, coffee, cakes, and I don't know what else. It would take me back forty years to see a cook roused at midnight, to prepare such a meal. I presume she even took herself to the roost and caught her young chicken by the legs and wrung its neck before she reached the newly-made fire. Major Haile knew we had not broken our fast at the town hotel.

It was late the following day when we all assembled to just as fine a breakfast, and heard the major say, "Your 'turnout' is gone. I sent to see about the condition of the creek; it goes down about as fast as it rises. When you are rested my carriage is at your disposal. Your driver was not used to these roads, but mine knows every crossing in the creek."

It was a four-mile drive, even after we had crossed the waters. The wedding house we found in commotion. There were no caterers or experts even in New Orleans in 1846. The wedding supper was in process of preparation, under the superintendence of a noted old cakemaker from Woodville, nine miles off. Everybody was busy; only General McCausland, the dear old master of the house, was quietly seated by his parlor window, a very old man, but a soldier withal, who could rise to emergencies when required. I drew up a chair and explained our delay, and told him how grandly hospitable his neighbor was. The two old men were the last remaining ones of their company of the battle of New Orleans. Their homes were in payment from the Government for their services. The dear old gentlemen said they were neither general nor major; they were simple soldiers who had discharged their services and accepted their pay. Both the men were

Irish, both poor boys. They worked hard, soon exhausted the old red soil of their neighborhood.

Later the General moved his workmen to the river bottoms, so that, while living for health's sake in the old home, the house of which he originally helped to build, his income came from Bayou Fordoche, many miles away.

Time flew; neighbors had arrived, the table was spread in the long back porch. The guests, many of them, lived miles and miles away, in common country roads, often through dense woods—a long drive under best circumstances, a perilous one at night, everybody waiting, everybody in a hurry, everybody getting tired and fretful. It was long after the appointed time, and the New Orleans preacher had missed the train! Old Dilsey in the kitchen was mad because her pig was getting too brown; Elfey in the porch worrying that her ice cream was waiting too long; ladies in the parlor trying to kill time; men wandering around the front yard in restless groups. Carriages had been to the depot; no appearance of Mr. Jahleel Woodbridge, the New Orleans minister. He was endeared to the family, had been for years their minister at Woodville. Bride, in all her regal attire, upstairs in tears; no Presbyterian preacher nearer than ten miles away. So we waited and waited. At last the General sent for his especial groom, ordered him to take the buggy and go four miles through the woods, where there was a Methodist itinerant, and tell him to come without delay to marry the couple.

The accommodating preacher came, just as he was. He had been plowing his field, and his wife, off to see a sick child, had carried the keys with her. He could not even get a clean handkerchief, but he came in his workaday suit. The company hastily assembled. He performed the ceremony, gave them his blessings, and congratulated her on her "escape from the quicksands and shoals of celibacy." Recognizing his own condition at the time, he begged to be excused from refreshments, and took a rapid and hurried departure. The kindly man was scarce gone when Mr. Jahleel Woodbridge arrived in a coach, most astonishingly like the one we had used the previous day. Only a year or two later the hospitable Major passed away; shortly after the General followed him, and the dear old homes have passed away also from the face of the earth.

XIV

THE BELLES AND BEAUX OF FORTY

DO not think I mean to imply the belles and beaux of which I am about to speak were forty years old, but they had their butterfly existence in the year 1840. Some, no doubt, fluttered around before, and a few after that date, but they all were of that era of simple life that, alas! is of the distant past—a host, as Auctioneer Beard used to say when parading his goods, "too multitudinous to particularize." In the first place, the costumes, as well as the customs of society, were so different from those of the present day that they marshal before my mind's eye almost like a fancy dress parade.

Miss Ellen Johnson, who became later the wife of William B. Walker (of the firm of Woodlief & Walker), and her sister, Malvina, wife of our celebrated Dr. Warren Stone, wore the most beautiful curls—wore them long after that style ceased to be *haut ton*. I have some "Moniteurs des Dames" of that early date that afford insight into costumes then worn. The long pointed waist, chuck full of real, hard, stiff whalebones (all the whalebones must have been used up then; nobody can find one now), corset also whaleboned to the limit, laced at the back and with literally a board up the front, at least three inches wide—a real board, apple tree wood preferred, hard and stiff and unyielding. Ladies so girded up walked and stood and sat, too, like drum majors; no round, stooping shoulders; one just had to stand straight, with an apple tree board as a constant reminder. I used even to hear that in cases where the poise had a tendency to lapse it was not unusual for the victim to wear the corset night and day.

The tournure of 1840 was buried in such oblivion that it requires one to be almost eighty years old to drag it forth and display its hideousness, explain its construction. The tournure, called "tchuny" for short, was long and round, the size and shape of the biggest kind of a rolling pin, such as your cook uses for pastry. The ends, however, tapered to points, which met and were secured in front of the waist. It was stuffed with moss, or cotton, or hair, I don't know what, for the monstrosity "came ready-made" from France. Over this awful precipice the full gathered dress skirt fell in rippling cascades. I remember a chiné silk, an indistinct, plaided purple and green; it was ruffled to the waist, and over the tchuny it hung in irregular folds. To my childhood's eye it was most graceful and beautiful. Good-by, tchuny! I am sure you will never resurrect. Your reign was disastrous to taste. You lived one short decade; without a mourner when you departed. Good-by, tchuny!

Whatever did become of chiné silks? Can it be possible they are back on the counters masquerading under another name? I never see a silk now that bears any resemblance to the pretty chiné of 1840. Nor do I see tarletans of that date. It required a whole piece (or bolt) of that goods for a dress. It had to have at least three skirts, one over the other, to give the diaphanous effect. Such sweet, simple dresses they were, too. Miss Mary Jane Matthews, a belle of the forties, wore a pink tarletan, trimmed with wreaths of small white roses, that was an inspiration. One very striking one comes to mind, gold colored, garnished with red hollyhocks! I think some Western girl must have sported that; it was scarcely simple enough for Creole taste.

Emma Shields was a noted beauty. I recall a plaster bust of Queen Victoria, idealized beyond all reason or recognition, one of my brothers kept on a shelf in his room. He adored it because he saw a resemblance to beautiful Emma Shields. She, poor girl, married unfortunately, and dropped suddenly out of sight. About the same time an accidental flourish of a feather duster knocked Queen Victoria off the shelf—and smashed my brother's idol.

Don't I recall as though he stood before me this minute, on my father's balcony, Mr. Peter Anderson? Tall and thin and angular (he imagined he looked like Henry Clay, and he was of similar build), dressed in what was known as moleskin, a tan-colored goods looking strangely like rough-finished kid, the trousers so skin-tight and so firmly strapped under the shoe that he had to assume a sitting posture with considerable deliberation and care.

Here comes Adolphus Hamilton, a quiet eligible, more known in business than in social circles, but the far-seeing mammas kept an eye on him, he was such a *bon parti*. One fine day he surprised these mammas by arriving with his bride from a trip to Natchez. Henry Hollister, too, was a business man who made few social calls, but was in evidence at all the dances. A few years ago I met his daughter at a summer resort. She was prodigiously amused that papa, now hobbling about with a gouty foot and stout cane, ever could have been a dancing beau.

George W. Kendall went off one fine day, to what he proposed would be a kind of picnic, in the wilds of Western Texas. His Santa Fe expedition spun out a longer and more varied experience than he contemplated, of which his graphic account, now unhappily out of print, is most entertaining. He married in France, and in Texas during the war we met him, after a lapse of many years. He had founded the town of New Braunfels, near San Antonio, and retired, full of years, and full of interest in the rough life around him, so different from the New Orleans of his earlier days and the Paris of his gayer ones.

The Miltenberger brothers were never old. They danced and made themselves admired through several generations of belles. The "sere and yellow leaf" could never be applied to a Miltenberger. Evergreens were they, game to the last, for no doubt they are all gone, and the places that knew them will know them no more.

A. K. Josephs, a lawyer of some note and a very acceptable visitor, was a replica in the way of flowered waistcoast and dangling chains of a prominent man of his race in England, Disraeli. Don't I see a bird of paradise waistcoat? Indeed I do. And also a waistcoat of similar style sent to another prominent beau of the period, a black satin confection, with gorgeous peacocks embroidered on the ample front. I don't think the recipient of that garment ever appeared in it. Flamboyant as were the waistcoats of that day, a peacock with spread tail was the limit. They are all dead, those belles and beaux of the forties. The old lady chronicler could expect nothing else of these folks she loves to remember and talk of to children and grandchildren, who listen with becoming patience, no doubt often thinking, "Dear grandma must be nearing her dotage."

XV

AS IT WAS IN MY DAY

I AM like the deaf old lady who, when asked why she took a box at the opera when she could not hear, replied, "I can see." So it is on piazzas at summer hotels, I do not overhear remarks, so perforce the pleasure of gossip is denied me, but "I can see," and no doubt do observe more than those who have the other faculty to play upon; also I see and moralize. Last summer in the mountains didn't I see young girls, young society girls, educated girls who ought to have known better, with bare heads and bare arms playing tennis in the hot sun; and, worse still, racing over the golf links? I could see them from my window, equally exposed, chasing balls and flourishing clubs. The sun in August is pitiless even on those breezy mountains, so I was scarcely surprised when one young girl was overcome by heat and exposure, and was brought to her mother at the hotel in a passing grocer's cart or lumber wagon. I tell my grandchildren who want to "do like other girls" that is not the way "other girls" did in my day. Grandma may be so old that she forgets, but she moralizes all the same. These athletic girls come back to city homes so sunburnt and with such coarse skin they have to repair to a skin specialist, and have the rough cuticle burnt off with horrid acids, and be polished up before the society season opens.

There are, of course, extremes, but years ago young ladies took more care of their complexions and of their hair, too. Years back of years, I don't know how they did. In my day we girls loved to visit the granddaughter of a voluble dame and listen to the old lady's talk, just like I am talking now. She thought we were criminally careless with our "skins," as she called it. Why, when she was young, her skin was so thin and clear that "one saw little blue veins meandering her neck." We always heard something as reminiscent in that house to laugh over till we saw the old lady again, and heard something equally remarkable of her youth. She was living in the past, as I am now, as I return to my experiences. One young girl visited me, ever so many years ago, who wore one of those awful, long, scoop sunbonnets all the time she was not at table or in bed. She looked like the proverbial lily. I used to wish she would take off that sunbonnet and say something, for she was dumb as a lily. I have entirely forgotten her name, though she was my guest for a whole stupid week; but I recall she was a relative or friend of the Morses. I don't know Mr. Morse's name; he was called Guncotton Morse, for he invented an explosive of that name, which the United States Government appropriated during the war.

Years after this young girl's visit to me I called on the charming Morse family in Washington. He was then urging his "claim." Every Southerner in Washington was after a "claim" at that time. I nearly broke my neck falling over a green china dog or a blue china cat in their dark parlor. Enterprising Morse barricaded himself behind his explosive, but I think he failed in his fight. I find I have wandered from the girls having their skins burned off to the Morses and their blue china cat! . . . In my days there were no specialists except cancer doctors. I think they always flourished—there were no skin specialists. A doctor was a doctor, nothing more nor less, and he was supposed to know all that was necessary of the "human form divine." He did, too, for people did not have the new-fangled diseases of to-day. A woman's hospital! Oh, heavens! Only last week I saw a friend, old enough to know better, but we never are so old we 'don't want to rid our faces of pimples and warts and wrinkles. This friend was a sight. I was really alarmed for her. She had been to a specialist. Her face was fiery red, all the skin removed by acid. Yesterday I saw her again, cured of sunburn and all the ills skin is heir to. Her complexion was that of the lily girl who wore the scoop sunbonnet. I do not advise you to try the experiment. It is shockingly painful, and does not always prove a success.

When I was a little girl, more than seventy years ago, mother made me, for summer romps in the country, gloves of nankeen, that well covered the wrist, had a hole for the thumb and a deep flap to fall over the hand. It was lucky they were easily made, and nankeen was not expensive, for I hated them and had a way of losing them in the currant bushes. Maybe you never saw nankeen? Gentlemen's waistcoats were often made of it, and little boys' trousers. If I lost my scoop sunbonnet one day—and it was surprising how easily I lost it! —it was sewed on the next. There were no such things as hatpins—and we had pigtails anyway, so they would have been of no use. Such tortures were inflicted when we were running wild over the blue grass farm, but no doubt the little Creole girls on the lakeshore were similarly protected. The hair specialist was not in evidence either.

Ladies had their hair done up with bandoline and

pomatums made of beef's marrow and castor oil and scented with patchouli; hair was done into marvelous plaits and puffs. A very much admired style which Henriette Blondeau, the fashionable hair dresser, achieved, was a wide plait surrounding a nest of stiff puffs. It was called the "basket of fruit." The front locks were tiny, fluffy curls each side the face and long ringlets to float over the shoulders. We all remember Henriette Blondeau. She dressed my sister's hair in the early forties, and she dressed mine ten years later, and I met her in

St. Louis Cemetery, New Orleans.

the hall of the St. Charles Hotel, plying her trade, twenty years later still, the same Henriette, with the same ample apron, the tools of her trade sticking out from her pockets. Now, almost forty years later still, she walks the streets of New Orleans no more. I hope she rests somewhere in the old French cemetery, for she knew and gossiped with so many who are taking their long sleep in that peaceful spot.

Mother made—no doubt your grandmother did, too—the pomade that was used on our hair. It was used, too, very freely; our locks plastered down good and smooth and flat. You may wonder how long hair so treated could last; just as long as hair ruffled the wrong way and marcelled with warm irons lasts our girls to-day. Mother's pomade was made of beef's marrow and castor oil. After the marrow was rendered to a fluid state, oil was added, then perfume, the whole beaten in a deep bowl until perfectly cold and white. Mother would beat and beat, add a few drops more of essence of bergamot, smell and smell and beat and smell, until she had to call a fresh nose to see if it was all right. I remember being told to try my olfactories on the soft, creamy stuff. A naughty brother gave my head a blow that sent my little pug-nose to the bottom of the bowl! My face was covered to the ears, and while mother scraped it with a spoon and scolded Henry, she was entreating me not to cry and have tears spoil her pomade. Maybe I might have forgotten how the stuff was made and how it looked, but for that ridiculous prank of the dearest brother ever was.

I have a sweet little miniature of that brother Henry, namesake of my father's dear friend, Henry Clay, with the queer collared coat and flourishing necktie of the day, and his long, straight hair well plastered with mother's good pomade. The dear man went to Central America, on a pleasure tour to the ruins of Uxmal in 1844. The vessel on which he sailed for home from Campeache, in September of that year, disappeared in the Gulf. We never had any tidings of how, or when, or where. I remember the firm of J. W. Zacharie was consignee of that ill-fated *Doric,* and how tenderly Mr. Zacharie came to my stricken mother, and how much he did to obtain information, and how for weeks after all hopes were abandoned my mother's heart refused to believe her boy was indeed lost. Every night for months she placed with her own trembling hands a lamp in the window of Henry's room, to light him when he came. She never gave up some remnant of hope. So far as I know, only one friend of that dear brother, one contemporary, is living now, in New Orleans. She is the last of her generation; I am the last of mine.

In those days there were few patent medicines, washes and lotions. There was a Jayne's hair tonic, and somebody's chologogue, that was a fever cure much in evidence on plantations, for quinine and blue mass pills—others, too—were made by hand. I have made many a pill. We had an old negro woman who was daft on the subject of medicine. There was not an earthly thing the matter with Hannah—she was just a chronic grumbler, begging for "any kind of pill." I doctored her successfully, making for her bread pills, rolling them in a little rhubarb dust to give them a nasty taste. They did her a world of good. Mother made our lip salve (didn't your grandmother?) of white wax and sweet oil. We did not have cold cream in those days.

When by accident, or some other way, our faces tanned, a wash overnight of sour buttermilk was all that was required. It was not very pleasant, and nobody wanted to occupy the room with you on sour buttermilk night. Reason obvious. Kentucky belles, who were noted for their rosy cheeks, often increased the bloom by a brisk rubbing of the leaves of the wild mullein. Except rice powder (and that is not a cosmetic) no cosmetics were in use.

Ve can recall at a later date than my girlhood a lady from somewhere up the coast married a finicky cotton broker in New Orleans. They made a wedding trip to Paris, and she returned with her face enameled. I don't think it could have been very skillfully done, for she had to be so careful about using the muscles of the face that she was absolutely devoid of expression. Once, in a moment of forgetfulness or carelessness, she "cracked a smile," which cracked the enamel. She returned to Paris for repairs. I saw her on the eve of sailing, and do not know if she ever returned.

XVI

FANCY DRESS BALL AT THE MINT IN 1850

I HAVE never heard of a society ball in a United States mint building, before nor since, but the Kennedys, who gave this one, were a power in the social world at that time—and ambitious beyond their means. Rose and Josephine, the two oldest of quite a flock of daughters, were débutantes that winter. Both were handsome and accomplished. Rose was also a famous pianist, even in those days when every woman strove to excel in music, and it was customary to entertain even a casual caller with a sonata. Gottschalk declared Rose Kennedy rendered his famous "Bamboula" better than he did himself, and to hear her was to rise and dance.

Who was at that fancy ball? Everybody who was anybody in the fifties. The Eustises—George and Mathilde, George as "a learned judge" (he was son of Chief Justice Eustis), and Mathilde in pure white and flowing veil was a bewitching nun. George, years after, married the only child of the banker-millionaire, W. C. Corcoran, in Washington.

Mathilde married Alan Johnson, an Englishman; both are long since dead. There was Mrs. John Slidell, of "Mason and Slidell" fame, a "marquise," in thread lace and velvet, her sisters, the Misses Deslonde, "peasant girls of France." Mathilde Deslonde became the wife of Gen. Beauregard, and her sister, Caroline, married Mr. R. W. Adams. All three sisters are with the departed. Col. and Mrs. John Winthrop, "gentleman and lady of the nineteenth century," the jolly colonel announced. Who fails to recall, with a smile, the Winthrops, who lived in Royal Street, near Conti; near neighbors of the—long departed—Bonfords? The genial colonel became a tottering old man, asking his devoted wife "who and where are we?" before he peacefully faded away. Young De Wolf of Rhode Island, nephew of Col. Winthrop's, "an Arab sheik," wore probably the only genuine costume in the room—a flowing robe that was catching in every girl's coiffure, and every man's sword and spurs, in the dance.

All the gilded youth who wanted boisterous fun, and no jury duty, were firemen, in those days of voluntary service. Philippe De la Chaise wore his uniform. He later married Victoria Gasquet, and was relegated to a "back number" shortly after.

I make no special mention of the chaperons, but,

Creole like, they were present in force. Cuthbert Slocomb was a *mousquetaire,* and Augusta, in red and black, "Diablotan," a vision of beauty and grace. She married the Urquhart mentioned in "Musical History of Louisiana," as the father of Cora Urquhart Potter. Mr. Urquhart died years ago, but his widow survives. She lives with her daughter at Staines on the Thames, in a stone house that was a lodge of Windsor Castle in the time of Henry VIII. Cuthbert Slocomb married a Miss Day; his widow and daughter, Countess di Brazza, survive him. Ida Slocomb was the noted philanthropist of New Orleans, the widow of Dr. T. G. Richardson.

There was the stately Mrs. Martin Gordon chaperoning her exceedingly pretty sister, Myrtle Bringier, who became the wife of Gen. Dick Taylor, and whose descendants are among the few of those mentioned above still living and reigning in New Orleans society.

The mint building was made ample for the gay festivities by utilizing committee rooms, offices and every apartment that could be diverted for the crowd's comfort—so, we wandered about corridors and spacious rooms, but never beyond the touch of a gendarme—officers, soldiers, policemen at every step. These precautions gave a rather regal air to the whole affair.

AUGUSTA SLOCOMB URQUHART
Painted in Paris, in 1857

FANCY DRESS BALL AT THE MINT IN 1850

The belles retired to their boudoirs for a season, but the beaux had to go to business, and what a sight some of them were for a whole week after the fancy dress ball! They had hired costumes from members of the French opera troupe, and their faces were "made up" with rouge that could not be washed off; had to wear off in a purplish stain. My brother represented Louis XIV on that occasion, and I remember he scrubbed his cheeks until he made them almost raw. Of no avail. In time the pinkish, purplish tint gradually disappeared.

Shortly after that grandest and most unique entertainment Mr. Joe Kennedy's term expired and he retired into private life. Beautiful Rose fell into a decline and died early. What fortunes befell that family I know not. They seem to have faded away. The Kennedys were a large family in those days, closely allied to the Pierce and Cenas families, all of which were socially prominent. And now their names are "writ in water." I should like to know how many of this old Creole society are living to-day! I was eighteen, one of the youngest of the group, in the fifties.

XVII

DR. CLAPP'S CHURCH

IT is quite sixty years since Dr. Clapp's church
went up in smoke. It was as well known to the
denizens and visitors of New Orleans, in its
day, as Talmage's Tabernacle in Brooklyn some
decades later was known far and wide. Dr. Clapp
called it "The First Congregational Church of New
Orleans." Others designated it as "Clapp's Church."
It was, in reality, neither one nor the other, for it
was not an organized congregation, and its building was the property of an eccentric Jew. In a
burst of admiration and generosity Judah Touro
gave the church rent free to Dr. Clapp. The structure had quite the appearance of a "Friends' Meeting House." It was of unpainted brick, entirely devoid of any ornamentation. The little steeple was
only high enough and big enough to hold the inevitable bell. One entered a narrow vestibule, with
two doors leading into the body of the church, and
two flights of stairs to respective galleries. It was
further furnished with two conspicuous tin signs—

"Stranger's Gallery on the Right," "Gallery for Colored Persons on the Left." (Dr. Clapp came from Boston.)

On entering the sanctuary one faced the organ loft, the pulpit being at the street end between the two doors. It was a little rounded affair, with, to all appearances, "standing room for one only." Back of it, to convey possibly an idea of space, and also to relieve the intense white of the wall, was a wonderful drapery, very high and very narrow, of red serge, pleated, looped and convoluted in an amazing way.

Dr. Clapp, a large, handsome, middle-aged man, in a clerical black silk robe, entered the pulpit from between the folds of that draped monstrosity. He was dignified and reverential, preached without notes, sometimes, but not always, using a Bible text. The music of that church was rated as very fine, the organ was the best in the city. (I wonder if old Judah Touro furnished that, too?) And Thomas Cripps, the organist, managed it, *con amore.* There must have been a choir to furnish the chorus, but I only call to mind Mrs. Renshaw and her sister, Miss White, who sang solos and duets. Their finely trained voices produced melody itself. Mr. James I. Day, tall, and thin, and gaunt, with a hatchet face, who looked as if a squeak was his vocal limit, had a most powerful bass voice that filled the building and floated out onto the street. The last time I saw him he was in an open carriage with a red velvet cushion on his lap, on which reposed the key (as big as the famous Bastile key) of the city of New Orleans. He was receiving Rex in an initial Mardi Gras parade. That was years ago.

To return to church, I don't recall any prayer books or hymnals, nor hearing any congregational singing. The choir, of course, was volunteer. We had yet to know a church singer could be salaried. There was no church organization, as we know it to-day, or even at that day. There were no officers, no deacons, no elders, far as I can think, for my father was a devoted communicant and constant attendant and naturally would have fitted into some church office, if there had been any.

When Dr. Clapp announced the taking of a collection he cast his eye over the congregation and signaled from it those persons who were to "pass the plates."

"Mr. Smith will take the center aisle, Mr. Jones the right aisle, Mr. Robinson the left aisle, Mr. Dick right gallery, Mr. Harry left gallery," whereupon Messrs. Smith, Jones and Robinson and Messrs. Dick and Harry would come forward, take their plates from a table under the high pulpit and proceed to their allotted tasks. Remembering this confirms me in the belief there were no officers of the church whose duty it would have been to discharge such services.

There was only one service a week, a morning service and sermon on Sundays, no night meetings, as there was really no means of lighting the building. No Bible class, no Sunday school, no prayer meeting, no missionary band, no church committee, no Donors' Society, no sewing circle, no donation party, no fairs, no organ recital, absolutely "no nothing," but Dr. Clapp and his weekly sermon. The church was always filled to its utmost capacity. I recall a host of pew holders whose names have passed into oblivion with their bodies.

The old church stood on St. Charles Street, adjacent to the St. Charles Hotel, so when one building went up in flames the other did, too. The Veranda Hotel, next in importance to its neighbor, was across the way, and from these sources always came strangers, more than enough to fill the gallery, when they were wafted up the stairs by the conspicuous tin sign.

Almost simultaneously with the destruction of the building, disappeared both Dr. Clapp and Mr. Touro from public notice. By the way, Mr. Judah Touro never had been inside the church, nor had he ever heard Dr. Clapp preach. Of course, they are both as dead now as the unique old church, so it matters not how, when or where they departed. The congregation dissolved as completely. Probably not one member, old enough at the time to know what Dr. Clapp preached about or to be able to criticise his utterances, is living to-day. Dr. Clapp was a loyal citizen, a charitable, kindly man, one of the few who voluntarily remained in the city and ministered to the stricken and buried the dead in the fearful epidemics that ravaged the land every two or three years. His counsel reached the flotsam of a great city, and his teachings bore fruit. He is gone now where church organizations are not considered, but the good works he wrought by his simple methods are placed to his credit.

XVIII

I THINK I can safely say I possess the first daguerreotype ever taken in New Orleans. An artist came there about 1840 and opened a studio (artist and studio sound rather grand when one views the work to-day). That studio was at the corner of Canal Street and Exchange Alley. The artist needed some pictures of well-known men for his showcase, so he applied to my father, who was of the "helping hand" variety. And dear Pa was rewarded with the gift of a picture of himself all done up in a velvet-lined case, which he brought home to the amazement and wonder of every member of the family, white and black. I look at it now with a grim smile. Dear Pa's cravat ends were pulled out and his coattail laid nicely over one leg, and his hand spread so that one could see he had five big fingers. His head had been steadied straight up in a most unnatural position, with a kind of callipers or steel braces, and he must have been told to "look up and smile" for a full minute.

125

We prize that daguerreotype for its antiquity, but I hope seventy years hence when another and another generation opens my "war album" they will not laugh at the quaint *cartes de visite* it contains, though I confess some of them begin to look rather queer already. They were all gifts of near and dear friends, most of them with autograph attachments, some of which were so flourishing that I had to subscribe the names and dates on the backs.

There are Mr. and Mrs. Jeff Davis, dated 1860, before he was President, you perceive. Though I have letters from both, I never saw either after that date. There's Gen. J. Bankhead Magruder, in full uniform, far and away the most picturesque of my collection. The first time we ever met Gen. Magruder was very soon after the capture of the *Harriet Lane* in Galveston waters. The Texans were wild and jubilant at the dashing feat, and when we reached Houston, all travel-stained and worn out, the city was in a ferment of excitement.

The General dearly loved to tell a good story, and the impediment in his speech, a drawling lisp, made him vastly amusing. In his office one day one of his aides was tinkling a banjo. A travel-stained individual called:

"Is the General in?"

"No," tinkle, tinkle.

126

"When will he be in?"

"Don't know," tinkle, tinkle.

"Will you tell him I called?"

"What name?" tinkle, tinkle.

"Smith."

"I think I have heard that name before," tinkle, tinkle. "What Smith?"

"Gen. E. Kirby Smith, young man!"

No tinkle followed that reply. The young aide almost swooned away. Gen. Magruder surrounded himself with Virginia gentlemen aides, who gave him infinite trouble, he said.

In the early fifties "we met by chance, the usual way," Major F. Ducayet. A party driving down the old Bayou road one Sunday heard that at Ducayet's there would be found a rare collection of wonderful fowls and poultry, and the owner was very gracious about showing his assortment to visitors. After a bit of hesitation we ventured to introduce ourselves. Mr. Ducayet received us most hospitably, showed us through his lovely grounds and gave us the history of his rarest feathered pets, presented the two ladies with choice bouquets and insisted upon our partaking of refreshments. During the conversation that ensued Mr. Ducayet said he would not be able to increase his fancy flock, all of which had been brought him from foreign parts by captains and sailors, as a change in the administration would remove him from the position in the Custom House he had held for years. One of the party at once asked him to call on him at the St. Charles Hotel the following day, that he, being a Democrat and a politician of influence, might exert himself in his behalf. Mr. Ducayet retained his position. From that chance acquaintance sprung a strong friendship. We saw much of Major Ducayet in war times, hence the little *carte de visite* which ornaments my war album.

By the side of Major Ducayet's is the face of ex-Governor Moore of Louisiana. He was an inmate of our modest little home in Texas during the expiring days of the Confederacy.

I have also similar small photos of Major Tom Lee, General Preston, General Breckinridge, Commodore John N. Maffit, General and Mrs. Robert Toombs, General Early, Dr. Howard Smith and a host of lesser lights, all of which were taken in Havana after the war.

Dr. Howard Smith of New Orleans was surgeon on somebody's (perhaps Gen. Kirby Smith's) staff, and was our frequent guest in Texas, a very valuable guest, too, for his skill carried some members of my family out of the "valley of the shadow" into the sunshine. One trip we made together from the Rio Grande into the interior of Texas, quite a caravan of us in the party.

The first day out from Laredo there was a terrible sandstorm, cold almost to freezing point, and never was a more disgusted party of travelers. In a fit of despair Dr. Smith exclaimed: "I would give a thousand dollars for a drink of brandy." Now brandy was a luxury a thousand dollars could not always supply, but I promptly replied: "I will give you a whole bottle of brandy, the cork of which has not been drawn, if you will divide it with the rest of the crowd." Of course, the proposition was accepted. From my carpetbag I produced a tiny toy bottle, holding perhaps a half wine glass of the coveted liquor. It was not easy to divide the contents liberally, but the genial doctor appreciated the joke and did his utmost to carry out its provisions.

Years after, walking uptown in New Orleans, my escort said: "Look at the man on that gallery. See if you know him." I met the man's eyes full in my face, and passed on. It was Dr. Howard Smith, neither of us recognizing the other. He was in ill-health, old and haggard, and I guess I showed some of time's footprints, too.

XIX

IN the twilight of my days, seated in my favorite chair, I rock away many a trip from my New Orleans home to the blue grass region of my ancestors. Dream trips they are, but dreams of real trips in the old days when steamboats and stages were the approved, in fact, the only, transportation for travelers.

About the Fourth of July every year our family migrated to the old Kentucky homestead. The Fourth was not chosen with any patriotic motive, but law courts were closed and legal business suspended, and my father's vacation at hand at that date. Though the steamboats were called palatial, viewed from my rocking-chair trip to-day I wonder how people managed to stand the inconveniences and discomforts they provided.

There was the famed *Grey Eagle*, "a No. 1 floating palace" it was called. There was the *Belle of the West* and the *Fashion* and the *Henry Clay*. One time and another we churned up the muddy Missis-

sippi water in every one of them. Naturally the
boats catered in every way to the predilections of
the plantation owners, who were their main source
of profit. The picture of Arlington which illustrates this book was originally made to decorate a
state-room door on a fine new river boat built in the
'50's and adorned in that way with views of homes
along the river.

STEAMBOAT ON THE MISSISSIPPI.
(From "Forty Etchings, from Sketches Made with the
Camera Lucida in North America in 1827 and 1828," by Captain
Basil Hall, R. N.)

Grey Eagle was the finest and best, and therefore
most popular boat. I recall with amusement an
eight or ten days' trip on that palace. The cabins
were divided by curtains, drawn at night for pri-
vacy. The ladies' cabin, at the stern, was equipped
with ten or twelve small staterooms. The gentlemen's cabin stretched on down to the officers' quar-

ters, bar, barber shop, pantries, etc., ending in what was called Social Hall, where the men sat about, smoking and chewing (the latter as common a habit as cigarette smoking is now) and talking—in other words, making themselves sociable.

On that same *Grey Eagle* I was for the first time promoted to the upper berth, in a stateroom shared by an older sister. The berth was so narrow that in attempting to turn over I fell out and landed in the wash basin, on the opposite side of the room! My sister had to sit on the lower berth to braid my pigtails, then sent me forth so she could have room to braid her own. Trunks and other baggage more unwieldy than carpetbags were piled up in the vicinity of Social Hall. A carpetbag, small enough to be easily handled, was all there was room for in the stateroom. There were no valises, suitcases or steamer trunks in those days of little travel, and unless you are three-quarters of a century old you can't imagine a more unwieldy article than a carpet-bag of seventy years ago. Only toilet articles and things that could not muss and tumble could be safely stored in one.

In the stateroom, where we had to sleep and dress, and, if we could snatch a chance, take an afternoon nap, there was a corner shelf for a basin and pitcher and one chair; two doors, one leading out and the other leading in, transoms over each for light and ventilation—and there you are for over a week. The cabin was lighted with swinging whale-oil lamps, and one could light his stateroom if one had thought to provide a candle.

Every family traveled with a man servant, whose business it was to be constantly at beck and call. Of course, there was always a colored chambermaid, and, equally of course, she frisked around and seemed to have very little responsibility—no bells, no means of summoning her from her little nodding naps if she happened to be beyond the sound of one's voice. The man servant's duties, therefore, were almost incessant. If an article was needed from the trunks he was sent to the baggage pile for it, and often he brought trunk trays to the staterooms. When the boat stopped "to wood" every man servant rushed to the woodman's cabin to get eggs, chickens, milk, what not.

And those men had the privilege of the kitchen to prepare private dishes for their white folks. I wonder how long a boat or hotel would stand that kind of management to-day; but in the days where my rocking-chair is transporting me, steamboat fare was not up to the standard of any self-respecting *pater familias*. There was no ice chest, no cold storage; in a word, no way of preserving fresh foods for any length of time, so passengers resorted to such means as presented themselves for their own bodily comfort. Those who had not the necessary appendage—a man servant—foraged for themselves, but the experienced and trusted servant, to use a vulgarism, "was never left."

The table for meals extended the length of the gentlemen's cabin, stretched out and out to its utmost length, if need be, so that every passenger had a seat. There was no second table, no second-class passengers—anybody was the equal of anybody else. If you could not possibly be that, you could find accommodation on the lower deck and eat from a tin plate.

It was quite customary, as I have mentioned, for passengers to have private dishes, prepared by their own servants. I recall with a smile, on one occasion, a very respectable-looking stranger boarded our boat at Helena or some such place. At dinner he reached for a bottle of wine. Cuthbert Bullitt touched the bottle with a fork, saying, "Private wine." The man, with a bow, withdrew his hand. Presently he reached for a dish of eggs. My father said, "Excuse me, private." There was something else he reached for, I forget what, and another fellow-passenger touched the dish and said "Private." Presently dessert was served, and a fine, large pie happened to be placed in front of the Helena man. He promptly stuck his fork into it. "By gracious! this is a private pie." There was a roar of laughter.

After dinner the others, finding him delightfully congenial and entertaining, fraternized with him to the extent of a few games at cards. He was wonderfully lucky. He left the boat at an obscure river town during the night, and the next day our captain said he was a notorious gambler. From his capers at table the captain saw he was planning a way of winning attention to himself, therefore under cover of darkness he had been put ashore. My father, who did not play, was vastly amused when he found the smart gambler had carried off all the spare cash of those who had enjoyed the innocent sport.

Flatboats floating all manner of freight down stream were a common sight on the river. Arrived at their destination, the boats, which were only huge rafts with no propelling power, were broken up and sold for lumber, and the boatmen traveled back up stream in packets to repeat the process. Cousin Eliza Patrick used to relate the trip her family made in about 1820 on a flatboat from Kentucky to Louisiana. The widowed mother wished to rejoin a son practicing medicine in the latter state, so she sold her land, and loaded her family and every movable object she possessed—slaves, cattle, farm implements, household effects—upon a huge "flat" and they floated by day and tied up to the bank by night, carrying on, during the weeks consumed by the trip, an existence which must have been somewhat like that of Noah's family in the Ark.

There was not, as I have mentioned, any means of keeping foods fresh, nor was there even ice water to be had on those boats. We used entirely, even for drinking, the muddy river water, which was hauled up in buckets on the barber side of the boat, while the steward was emptying refuse to the fishes on the pantry side. The passengers became more or less intimate, necessarily, on a trip such as I am attempting to describe. There was no place to sit but in the general cabin, the sleeping rooms being so cramped. There was no library, very little reading, but much fancy work, mostly on canvas, footstools and bell-pulls. A bell-pull, you may want to know, was a long band about three inches wide; it was hung from the parlor cornice and connected with a bell in the servant's region; it was quite the style to embroider them in gay vines and flower designs.

The elderly ladies knit fine thread nightcaps, collars and lace. Really some of the "old lady" work was quite handsome. Thus fingers were kept busy, while gossip and interchange of bread and cake recipes entertained the housewives who had never heard of cooking schools and domestic science. Our trip necessarily embraced at least one Sunday. I remember my father had a dear old relative of the

AMERICAN STAGECOACH.

(From "Forty Etchings, from Sketches Made with the Camera Lucida in North America in 1827 and 1828," by Captain Basil Hall, R. N.)

deepest dyed Presbyterian type (father of the late Dr. T. G. Richardson), who always on his river trips landed wherever he happened to be on Saturday and on Monday boarded another boat (if one came along), his scruples forbidding Sunday travel.

Arrived at the end of our river journey, father chartered a whole stage to take his family a two days' trip into the heart of the blue grass region. Nine passengers filled the interior of the coach, and four or five, if need be, could ride on top. The rumble (we always called it boot) was filled with baggage. The vehicle had no springs, but was swung on braces, which gave it a kind of swaying motion that always made me sick. However, we managed to start off in fine style, but every time there was a stop to change horses all of us alighted, stiff and tired and hot, to "stretch our legs," like Squeers in Dickens' "Nicholas Nickleby." At noon we rejoiced to hear our coachman's horn, a grand, loud blast, followed by toot, toot!—one toot for each passenger, so the tavern man would know how many plates to lay, and his wife how many biscuits and chicken legs to have ready. We always made out to spend the one night of the journey at Weissiger's tavern in Frankfort, the best tavern in all the land. We had a leisurely breakfast the following morning and were refreshed in body and soul for the last lap of our journey.

Late afternoon the stage winds up a hill, and in a woods pasture and surrounded by blue grass meadows the gable end of a red brick house can be seen. My dear, tired mother puts her head out of the window, "Driver, blow your horn." A great blast sounds over the waving grass and blossoming fields, and we know that they know we are coming. Tired as the horses are after the long, hard pull; tired as the coachman must be, he cracks his whip, and we gallop up the shady lane to the dear old door as briskly as though we were fresh from the stable. Long before we are fully there, and the steps of the nine-passenger coach can be lowered; long before the boys can jump off the top, a host of dear faces, both white and black, is assembled to greet us. As a little child I always wondered why it was, when the occasion was so joyful, and all of us tumbled from that stage so beaming and happy, that as my aunt folded my mother in her arms, they both wept such copious tears. Now I know.

XX

HOTEL AT PASS CHRISTIAN IN 1849

IF there is a more restful spot on earth than a
comfortable rocking-chair on a deep veranda,
with a nearby view of the dancing waters of the
gulf through a grove of tall pines, commend me to
it. A whole month on the west coast of Florida, all
sand underfoot, pines and oaks overhead, is ideal
for fagged-out, tired-out, frayed-out humanity from
busy cities. This is not an advertisement, so I do
not propose to tell where six people from six different and widely separated parts of the country
last year dropped down from the skies, as it were,
upon just such a delightful straight mile of gulf
coast.

One halts at a "turpentine depot" and takes
a queer little tram to the Gulf, seven miles away.
Tram is hauled over wooden rails by two tired nags
whose motions suggest the lazy air of the pines. It
is loaded with the baggage—crates of hunting dogs
—(fine hunting abounds), the mail bag, some miscellaneous freight and finally the passengers.

HOTEL AT PASS CHRISTIAN IN 1849

The country hotel is pine; ceilings, floors, walls are pine, the home-made and built-in furniture is pine; a big fire, roaring in the open fireplace if the day is chilly, is also made of pine—the rich, red Florida pine, ever so much richer in color and in turpentine than the boasted Georgia article. With the fish swimming in front of this hotel and the birds flying behind, and rabbits running in both directions, it goes without saying the table is above the average.

Here on the broad verandas, as we rock and dream the lazy days away, visions visit me of the old hotel at Pass Christian in the forties. The oaks and three China trees in front of the veranda, and the view of the near-by waters, the whistle of mocking-birds among the china berries (thank heaven! sparrows have not found this Elysium) lend additional force to the semblance. One old lady, who hunts not, neither does she fish, rocks on the sunny veranda and dreams, as is the wont of those who have lived beyond their day and generation. She brings forth from a long-forgotten corner of memory's closet a picture covered with the dust of years, and lovingly brushes away the dimness, when behold! old Pass Christian, dear old Pass Christian, before the day of railroads and summer cottages, before the day of 6 o'clock dinners and trailing skirts, of cotillion favors and abbreviated bathing suits.

The old hotel was built with a wing or extension at each end, which formed with the main building three sides of a square. There was no attempt at landscape gardening; not even a rosebush or an oleander decorated the little court. No plaster Apollos and Dianas such as were seen peeping about the shrubbery of the various cottages (like the De Blancs' and Ducayets') that dotted in those days the old bayou road, and were considered so very decorative, but plain sand and scrub such as meet my eye to-day on this little frequented part of the Florida Gulf Coast. There was no beach driving or riding of gay people then—none here now.

I fly back to the summer of '49, and live again with the ·young girls who made life one long summer's day. We walked the pier, the image of one before my eyes now, to the bath-houses in muslin dresses. Bathing suits were hideous, unsightly garments, high neck, long sleeves, long skirts, intended for water only! The young girls returned under parasols and veils. How decorous! No *baigneuse decolletée* to be seen on the beach. Our amusements were simple and distinctly ladylike. There was no golf or tennis, not even the innocent croquet, to tempt the *demoiselles* to athletics, so they drifted more to the "Lydia Languish" style.

There was no lack of beaux who came, more than enough to "go round," by the Saturday boats, in time for the weekly hop—danced all Saturday night and returned to weekly drudge (as they called it) in the city. The bonbons and flowers they brought vanished and faded long before the little boat with its freight of waving hats and handkerchiefs faded in the twilight of a summer Sunday.

Also there come to my dream two dainty Goodman sisters, wonderful and most accommodating musicians they were. One was already affianced to her cousin, George Nathan. He was a prosperous business man at that time. I doubt if even his name is known among his thrifty race in New Orleans to-day. He carried off his accomplished wife to Rio Janeiro, and made his home in that country, which was as far away to us then, as the North Pole is to-day. The younger sister met that summer at the Pass and eventually married E. C. Wharton, an attaché of the *Picayune,* whose articles were signed "Easy Doubleyou." He was soon dancing attendance on the pretty, curly haired girl. I remember how he wandered around with pad and pencil, and we girls were horribly afraid of being put in the *Picayune.* No reason for fear, as it was before the dawn of the society page and personal column. The Whartons drifted to Texas during the war, and at Houston they found already a host of stranded Louisianians; but "Easy Doubleyou" had a government appointment of some kind. The rest of us were simply runaways.

There, too, was Dick Taylor, propelled in a wheel chair over that hotel veranda, an interesting convalescent from severe illness, or perhaps a wound, I do not recall which, his valet so constant in attendance that we wondered how the young man ever got an opportunity to whisper sweet nothings into the ear of lovely Myrtle Bringier—but he did! And that was the fourth engagement of the season that culminated in marriage, which signalizes the superior advantages of a hotel veranda, and most especially that of dear old Pass Christian. Dick Taylor had a magnetic personality, which overshadowed the fact (to paraphrase a Bible text) he was the only son of his father, and he the President.

In New York some years ago "The Little Church Around the Corner," still garnished with its wealth of Easter lilies and fragrant with spring bloom, threw wide its portals for the last obsequies of this loved and honored Confederate general. In that throng of mourners was one who had known him in his early manhood on the veranda of that old

Pass Christian hotel, and whose heart had followed his career with ever-increasing admiration and veneration even unto the end. I lay aside my old picture forever. Alas! it remains "only a dream at the best, but so sweet that I ask for no more."

XXI

OLD MUSIC BOOKS

I WONDER how many old ladies start to go through an unused hall closet, to make room for an accumulation of pasteboard boxes too good to throw away, and hampers too strong to discard, and in that long-closed closet, which a junk man with push-cart is waiting to help clear out, find a treasure, long since buried under piles of trash, mourned for, and, as in the case of many departed things, at length given up for lost—then forgotten. In just such a dark closet, from beneath a pile of old magazines (what they were kept and stored for goodness knows) and crazy bits of bric-a-brac, that nobody but a junk man (not even Salvation Army men, who are getting to be mighty choosy, by the way) would cart off, I found two bruised music books.

One dated back to 1847, when I was a schoolgirl in New Haven, and played with great éclat "La Fête au Couvent" quadrilles, purchased of Skinner & Co., Chapel Street. Chapel Street still exists, but Skinner & Co. are buried in the dust of more than sixty years. I cannot play "La Fête au Couvent" or any other fête now, but I can close my eyes and see the lovely young girls in the school music room whirling away to the music of the inspiring cotillion. Alas! Alas! Time has whirled every one of them away and stiffened the nimble fingers that danced so merrily over the keys.

In those far away days that are as yesterday to my dreaming there were "Variations" of every familiar melody. Variations that started with the simple air and branched off into all sorts of fantastic and involved and intricate paths. "Oft in the Stilly Night," " 'Tis Midnight Hour," "Twilight Dews," "Low-Back'd Car," "The Harp That Once Thro' Tara's Halls," "Oh, Cast That Shadow From Thy Brow," and so on and on, whole pages of "Variations," now dim with age, but every blessed note brings to me the faces and voices of those long stilled in death. One sweet young girl played "The Harp That Once Thro' Tara's Halls" and " 'Tis Midnight Hour" so charmingly that my eyes were dimmed when I turned the leaves of the school-day music book, for her fate was saddest of all—an inmate for years of an insane asylum. Another who sang as she played the "Low-Back'd Car" so delightfully (she was half Irish) died suddenly of yellow fever. Still another associated with "Oh, Cast That Shadow From Thy Brow," played the melody on a guitar, accompanied by her sweet young voice. Alas! She, too, is gone where they play on harps and there are no shadowed brows. So, on and on to the bitter end, and with a sigh I close the first chapter of my musical reminiscences that have lain dormant so many, many years.

The fashion of dedicating bits of music to some well-known person—need not be a musician, either, but a body of some note—has passed away with the one-button glove and the green *barège* veil of sixty years ago. In the '50s it was quite common, and my dear music book of that date holds ever so many dedicated polkas and mazourkas. The very front leaf has a picture of a wonderfully crocheted kind of a serpent with a man's head, rather a shocking thing, "Sea Serpent Polka," dedicated to Miss Rose Kennedy, by M. Strakosch. Dear Rose used to play it for us. It was not an inspiring bit of music, but her wonderfully deft touch would make melody out of anything that had crochets and quavers in it.

There is, a few pages further, another dedication to the incomparable Rose, "Grande Polka de Concert," by Wallace. Miss Lou Gross, a most accomplished musician, daughter of the noted surgeon, Dr. Samuel Gross, was honored by Strakosch in the

"Kossuth Galop," a galloping thing, much in the Strakosch style, which predominated in those days. Strakosch believed in a grand "send off" of his innumerable productions. There's "Carnival de Paris," dedicated to Mme. Caroline Arpin (I did not know of her) and "Flirtation Polka," to Mme. Lavillebeuvre, who was a delightful pianist and merited something more inspiring than that "Flirtation."

Then Wallace dances on the pages with a "Polka" adorned with the name of Mlle. Dumilatre, and Ed Armant dedicates "La Rose Polka" to Miss Augusta Slocomb. I don't think Armant wrote music; he "got it done," as the saying is. That was not an unusual feat; a valse was dedicated to Miss Philomène Briant, by George McCausland, and he was ignorant of a note in music—he "got it done." P. A. Frigerio honored Miss Sara Byrne by the dedication of "La Chasse Polka." Miss Sara was a decided belle in the '50s, so a bit of music with her name attached found rapid disposal. Also, a belle of the '50s was Miss Estelle Tricou. Lehman, *chef d'orchestre* at the opera house, wrote "Souvenir de Paris" in her honor. Miss Estelle was bright and sparkling and beautiful, so was much in evidence. George W. Christy wrote more than one of his "starry" verses to "E. T.," and they were printed in the *Picayune*. George was not noted for self-effacement and modesty. His signature always appeared in full to his sentimental effusions.

Lehman dedicated his "Clochettes Polka Mazourka," a fine, inspiring bit of dance music it was, too, to Mme. Odile Ferrier, and "La Valentine Polka," another charming, catchy dance piece, to Miss Anaïs Boudousquie. There was Mme. Angèlina, a new French importation, whose specialty was the new dances that nobody else could teach. She was immortalized by "L'Esmeralda Nouvelle Danse de Salon." We pupils had to learn some new steps and flourishes to be able to make successful début, after All Saints' Day, for it was decreed "L'Esmeralda" was to be most popular. Everybody, even some stout old ladies that did not mean to be relegated to back seats, and *passé* beaux who were fast becoming clumsy and awfully hard to dance with, took dancing lessons on the sly of Mme. Angélina, not to mention the young girls, débutantes and such, that went in small installments to her tiny room in Royal Street. . . . .

After this seeming digression I turn a leaf in the old music book to dedications to Mme. Boyer, "Mazourka Sentimentale," by the fertile Strakosch, and here, too, "La Valse Autrichenne" by a new name—E. Johns. Mme. Boyer was the

fashionable teacher of music. Both these dedicated
pieces we scholars had to learn, and both bits, besides a dozen other bits a thousand times more dif-
ficult and intricate, like Gottschalk's "Bamboula,"
for instance, are so spotted with black pencil marks
they are a sight! For the madame did not make a
suggestion as to technique or expression or anything else in the musical mind that was not emphasized by a pencil mark on the page.

I find that most of this music was published by
Mayo, No. 5 Camp Street; by Lyler & Hewitt, 39
Camp Street. Lehman published his own work at
194 St. Anne Street. . . . I am not half through,
but I am weary of looking over these old music
books. So many memories cluster about every page
—memories of lovely dances with delightful partners. Oh! That grand *valse à cinq temps,* the music
of which was never printed, and no band but Lehman's band could play it, and nobody taught the
whirling steps but Mme. Angélina. Memories of
sweet girls, now old and faded, or, better than that,
listening to the "Music of the Spheres." Memories
of painstaking professors whose pencil marks are all
that is left to bring forcibly to mind their patient
personality. I turn the last leaf, and lo! here is a
unique bit of music and information—"The Monterey Waltz," by Eugene Wythe Dawson, a little

Texas boy, who dedicates it to the little musicians of his own age (eight years) in the sister States! I do not remember anyone who essayed to render the "Monterey Waltz"—I never did—but Eugene Dawson was still playing the piano in Texas during the war, proving possibly our grandfather's dictum, "A man who plays the piano is mighty little account for anything else."

We don't think so now. I would be glad for a musician, male or female, in this house to render for me the sweet musical numbers that once made my young heart bound.

XXII

THE SONGS OF LONG AGO

HOW the ballads of our youth are, in memory, merged into the personality of those who sang them! How, as we recall the simple rhymes, the sweet voices of departed friends clothe them in melody. The songs of my early years come to me to-day with more freshness than the songs I heard yesterday, and with them come more vividly to mind the voices and faces of those long-gone friends than come the faces of those of to-day.

How many of us can recall "Blue-eyed Mary"? the little ballad with which my mother always quieted me to rest. The pitiful little song! And in my childhood days, too, mammy rocked me to sleep with "Ole Grimes is daid, dat good ole man." I never hear "Blue-eyed Mary" or "Old Grimes" now, nor have I for more than threescore years and ten, they are both so buried in oblivion, though I can repeat every word of each, they were so nestled and rocked into my baby life.

When my father's home was on Customhouse Street Duncan Hennen lived directly opposite. Mrs. Hennen was a dashing beauty. She had a sister from Tennessee visiting her, who had a powerful voice, and she sang "Old Rosin the Beau" and "Life on the Ocean Wave" with all the abandon of a professional. My father admired her style prodigiously, but my mother thought it too robust. "The Carrier Dove—fly away to my native land, sweet dove," and "Twilight Dews," she pronounced more ladylike. (How often we used that word "ladylike." We rarely hear it now.) I must have been a very small "little girl" when I heard Wallace, in concert, sing "The Old Arm Chair." No one since Wallace ever sung that touching, homely ballad so beautifully. Once having heard his sympathetic rendering, one always associates the song with William Wallace.

I think it has been full sixty years since that song and "Farewell to Tom Moore," by Byron, have been heard. And "Twilight Dews," oh, my! and "Shells of the Ocean"—"One summer's day in pensive thought," etc. Young girls played their accompaniments and tossed their ringlets and sang those ditties to enraptured swains, who often stood back of them, holding the candle at the proper angle and turning the leaves! How it all comes back to this dreaming old lady, who never sang, but who dearly loved to listen to her more gifted friends. . . . .

In the Cajin settlement on the border of which I occasionally visited there was a family of Lafitons— I boldly give the name, for the two sons, Lafiton *fils* and Pete, never married, and all the family died years and years ago, but there was a lovely sprig of a girl, Amenaide, who possessed a fine voice and no doubt would have made her mark if she had had the necessary training, but she was one of the flowers "born to blush unseen." I don't think she knew one note of music. Of course, a guitar, much more a piano, was beyond her reach. She sang the sweet old French melody, "Fleuve du Tage," delightfully. I wonder now where she ever heard it. For years after when I heard the song Amenaide rose before me, and with her the impression that she was not equaled.

There was another touching little ballad, in the days that were, "We Have Been Friends Together," and that tender "Good-by," who ever sings them now? Nobody, unless it be some old lady with quavering voice, who sings them in her heart while she dreams of the sweet girls of "Long, long ago" who have vanished.

"I Cannot Sing the Old Songs," and "When Stars Are in the Quiet Skies" were two of the songs we loved to hear in the days before "Dixie" and "The Volunteer" and "The Bonnie Blue Flag" captured the voices of so many of our sweet singers.

Some of us remember Mollie Haynes, who became the wife of Col. Charles D. Dreux, and none can recall her charming personality without a thought of the superb voice she possessed. "Ave Maria, Ora Pro Nobis"—none that I knew could render that prayerful melody with the pathos of Mollie Dreux. We all remember that Col. Dreux was the first Confederate officer from Louisiana who fell in battle, and no subsequent funeral was more largely attended than was Charles Dreux's. "Joys That We've Tasted" brings to mind a popular singer in the "Long Time Ago," Mrs. George D. Prentice, of Kentucky. How the names and the very people come thronging my mind as I recall these old melodies in which they are associated.

A few years since, listening to the well-trained voice of a professional, as she rendered some intricate, superlative kind of music, that did not in the least appeal to me, I ventured to ask if she would favor us with "Ben Bolt." She graciously consented. And she rendered that simple old ballad that every child whistled or hummed when I was a child, with so many trills and bravuras, and I don't know what else in the vocal line, that I was lost in amazement.

Svengali himself could not have idealized to the same extent. Poor "Sweet Alice" was buried under such an avalanche of sound that one could not recognize the "corner, obscure and alone," where she was supposed to rest under a "slab of granite so gray."

So, perhaps, in the march of improvement, where none sing unless they possess a voice that would electrify a whole opera house audience, it is well the dear old songs of long ago are not resurrected and amplified to suit the tastes and requirements of to-day. I recall though, with a thrill of tender memory, hearing Jenny Lind sing "Home, Sweet Home"—just the simple ballad—without a single flourish when she was in New Orleans in 1851. I was in deep mourning and did not dream I would have the pleasure of hearing her, but a friend secured a *loge grillée,* and insisted upon my going, accompanied by my brother. It was all arranged so courteously and so sympathetically and so kindly that I could not refuse, and thus I heard that incomparable artist sing "Home, Sweet Home."

No longer can mother sit in her "old arm chair" waving a turkey tail fan warm summer evenings, and be comforted and soothed by sweet warblings of her girls at the piano. No longer can the tired father call for his favorite, "Oh! Would I Were a

Boy Again," or "Rock Me to Sleep, Mother," **or** Mrs. Hemans' "Bring Flowers, Fresh Flowers," the sweet old flowers that all girls were singing sixty years ago. The old mothers and fathers, the bright young daughters are scarce buried more deeply or mourned more deeply than are the songs of long ago.

XXIII

A RAMBLE THROUGH THE OLD CITY

IN the days of which I write New Orleans bore a very different aspect from the present, and it may be well for me to take my readers on a gossipy ramble through the thoroughfares which I so often traverse nowadays in my thoughts.

Canal Street in the early forties was, par excellence, a resident street. From Camp and Chartres Streets, way back as far as sidewalks were flagged or bricked, which was only a few blocks, Canal Street was lined with homes, side by side, often without even an alley to separate them, as though land was scarce and one need economize space, whereas just beyond was land in plenty, but no sidewalks or easy approaches to speak of. From Camp Street to the levee were as I remember, large wholesale business houses, convenient to the shoppers of large supplies, who arrived at regular intervals from their plantations on *Belle Creole,* or some other coast packet, frequently retained their quarters on the boat the short time it was in port, and so monsieur and madame could accomplish their necessary shopping, untrammeled by the elegancies and inconvenient hours of a hotel.

Things were conducted on a very liberal basis in those days. I have a liking for that old way—it was so debonair and generous, putting the captain on the same social standing as his guests.

On the lower side of Canal Street, about where Holmes' store now stands, were more homes, in a row, all the houses exactly alike, with narrow balconies stretching clear across the fronts, in a most confidentially neighborly way. The lower floors were doctors' or lawyers' offices or exchange brokers'. Fancy goods, dry goods, retail shops, in fact of every kind, were on Chartres or Royal Street; none on Canal. R. W. Montgomery had his home also on that fashionable thoroughfare.

Christ Church was on the corner of Baronne and Canal, and Dr. Laycock was the pastor at the date of which I write, and, with few exceptions, all these families were of his flock.

Lower Camp Street was occupied mostly by exchange brokers' and such offices. The Sun Mutual Insurance Company had a conspicuous sign on a modest two-story brick building which any insurance structure to-day would put to shame.

If it is near Christmas time, when we are taking this gossipy ramble, we might meet a flock of turkeys marching up Camp Street, guided by a man and boys with long poles. In those days fowls were not offered for sale ready dressed or plucked, but sold "on the hoof," as we say of cattle. Camp and the adjacent resident streets were, to use another Westernism, a favorite "turkey trot." Those turkeys may have trotted miles. Goodness knows whence they took up the line of march—presumably at some boat landing—but they were docile as lambs and in good condition. No roast turkey gobbler, or, better still, boiled turkey hen with oyster dressing, tastes now like the ones mother had on her table when I was a child and clamored for the drumstick. What does taste as good to us old folks to-day? Nothing! Absolutely nothing! . . . .

In Exchange Alley (it may have a new name now, since Triton Walk and Customhouse Street and others of the old days have been rechristened) my father and a number of other "attorneys at law," as their signs indicated, had offices. Mr. Wharton was one, and I also recall two Hebrew beaux of that date who were neighbors of my father's, A. K. Josephs and M. M. Cohen. Nobody knew their given names. Beyond Camp Street, near Magazine, Mme. Shall kept a boarding house. It was a popular hostelry for gentlemen. Ladies did not board, except (to use Susan Nippers' language) as temporaries.

Visitors to the city "put up" at the St. Charles Hotel, in the hands of Colonel Mudge. St. Charles was the best hotel even then, comparing favorably with the Galt House, in Louisville, under the management of that prince of hosts, Major Aris Throckmorton—which is saying volumes for the St. Charles. In the season flocks of Nashville, Louisville and Cincinnati belles descended upon New Orleans, sat in gorgeous attire and much chatter of voices on the divans under the chandelier of the St. Charles parlor, while the kindly fathers and insinuating brothers, bent on giving the girls a good

EXCHANGE ALLEY.

time, foraged about the ample rotunda, captured, escorted in and introduced many eligible beaux found sauntering around that fascinating rendezvous.

Up Carondelet Street—one could not find the location on a city map now, for, as I remember, the streets were not named—were suburban homes, all about, quite remote and countrified. Judge John N. Duncan lived in one of those cottages. There was a grand, big yard surrounding it, with fig trees, hedges, rosebushes and vines, a perfect bower of delight to us children. Rose, the only daughter, was a lifelong friend of mine. She became the first wife of Col. William Preston Johnston. Nearby lived the Peter Conreys, who gave lovely lawn parties, that the naughty uninvited dubbed "Feat sham peters."

Not so very far away, in the neighborhood of Constance and Robin Streets, there was erected in 1843 quite a grand residence for the Slark family. I do not remember much of them in those early days, though they lived near enough to my father's to be neighbors. Later in life my acquaintance with them was more intimate. I recall, though, quite vividly Mrs. Slark's visiting card, which I admired prodigiously. Being a small collector of curios that unique bit of pasteboard was one of my treasures till I lost it! There seems to have been considerable latitude in the style of visiting cards about that time

—some were highly glazed and had gilt edges; some were even pink tinged, but I think Mrs. Slark's was the *ne plus ultra*—a bird's beak holding a waving pennant, and on its flowing folds was engraved "Mrs.—Abigail—L.—Slark," something after the style of the eagle and *E pluribus unum.*

I find I am wandering away from that dear old Canal Street of fragrant memories. Fragrant, though the broad neutral ground was a wilderness of weeds of dampy growth, and (so our John used to tell me) snakes! There certainly were frogs after a spring rain. I have heard their croaks. Further back toward the swamps were deep ditches, with crawfish sneaking about in them. Fine fishing place for us little ones it was, too. After a heavy downpour of rain the poorly paved street and the low, marshy neutral ground was often flooded clear across from sidewalk to sidewalk. It was great fun to watch the men trying to cross the street after one of these rains. Rubber shoes were unknown, so men depended on high boots. Of course, ladies did not venture forth at such times, when they required more protection for the foot than a thin-soled slipper afforded. There were goloshes, wooden soles fastened with straps and buckles over the instep. A golosh looked like a roller skate and was about as easy to walk with. You never see one now.

A RAMBLE THROUGH THE OLD CITY

I wonder if anyone under seventy-five years of age passes old "Julia Street row" to-day and knows that those "13 Buildings" between Camp and St. Charles Streets have an aristocratic past, and were once occupied by the leading social element of the American colony residing in the early forties above Canal Street? "13 Buildings" it was called, and at that date, and a decade later, every one of them was tenanted by prominent citizens of New Orleans. There they lived and entertained a host of delightful guests, whose names were a power then, but whose descendants are perhaps little known to-day.

There lived Mr. Lanfear with his two daughters. Louisa later became the wife of David Ogden. There lived Mrs. Slocomb and her three children. They became Mrs. T. G. Richardson, so well known and honored to-day in the Crescent City; Mrs. David Urquhart, now living in England, and Capt. Cuthbert Slocomb. Late in the forties that family went to Europe, and returned to occupy the house, built in their absence, which is now the home of Mr. Frank Howard, opposite Lafayette Square.

The Branders—Mr. Brander was a merchant of some note and social standing. His daughter, Caledonia, married Mr. Sager, an Englishman, and eventually went to Europe. Virginia Brander became the wife of Edward Matthews, a New York

167

man, who subsequently made a large fortune by speculating in long leases of valuable business sites in New York during a panic in commercial circles at the time of the Civil War. Their son, Brander Matthews, is a distinguished man of letters and professor in Columbia· College. The Smith family, a host of handsome girls, occupied the house next to the Camp street corner, and in that house the original J. P. Labouisse married beautiful Dora Smith, whose death, at the advanced age of ninety, occurred a short time ago. Charles Cammack married Sarah Smith in the same house, and Mary Smith married Morris, the son of Beverly Chew, who was a defendant in the noted Gaines case of that day.

H. S. Buckner's home was midway of the row, and there was born Ellen Buckner, who became the wife of James B. Eustis, the first United States ambassador to France. Those old friends who visited Paris in her *régime* tell of her cordial and gracious hospitality.

Leonard Mathews lived in one of the "13 Buildings." He was agent of the Sun Insurance Company. There were young people in that house, too. Mary Jane Mathews married Mr. Hugh Wilson, a prominent business man, and their daughter married Lyman Josephs of Rhode Island. There was also the family of Dr. William Kennedy. Mrs. Kennedy

HENRY CLAY

was sister of Mr. Levi Peirce and of Mrs. Hillary Cenas. Their daughter, Charlotte, married a son of the distinguished Sargent S. Prentiss of Mississippi.

Diagonally across the corner of Julia and St. Charles Streets was the home of Col. Maunsel White, a veteran of Chalmette, who won his title on the field. A genial Irishman, his serenity was disturbed about the time of which I write by the elopement of his oldest daughter, Eliza, with the dashing Cuthbert Bullitt. She died many years ago, but Mr. Bullitt lived and dashed many years after dashing ceased to be becoming. A short time ago he also passed away at a ripe old age, having survived every contemporary.

My personal recollections of the guests who came to my father's house in "13 Buildings" are distinct. Henry Clay, a lifelong friend of father's, the only one I ever heard call him "Dick" (even my mother did not do that), was a frequent visitor whenever he came to the Crescent City.

My father planned in 1844 to go to England, and his old friend gave him the following letter. It was never delivered, owing to the enforced abandonment of the plan, and hangs now on my library wall, framed, beside the Henry Clay portrait which illustrates this book and which is by far the best likeness I have ever seen of Kentucky's gifted son.

ASHLAND, 16th July, 1844.
MY LORD:
Richard H. Chinn, Esq., who will deliver this letter desiring the honor of your Lordship's acquaintance, I take pleasure in introducing him (sic) to you as an eminent and highly respectable councillor at law, now residing in New Orleans, whom I have long known.

I avail myself of the opportunity to assure your Lordship of the constant esteem and regard of
Your Lordship's faithful and obedient servant,
H. CLAY.
THE RIGHT HONORABLE LORD ASHBURTON,
London.

Gen. E. P. Gaines and his tiny, frisky wife, the noted Myra Clark Gaines, were also frequent guests. The General, a warrior, every inch of him, very tall, erect and pompously stately, always appeared at "functions" in full uniform, epaulettes, sword and what not, while she, all smiles and ringlets and flounces, hung upon his arm like a pink silk reticule. There also came Charles Gayarré, the Louisiana historian; John R. Grymes, the noted lawyer; Pierre Soulé, diplomat; Alec Bullitt, Alec Walker and George W. Kendall—all three editors of the leading paper of the day, the *Picayune*. And so on, including a host of others just as noted and interesting in their day, whose names are never mentioned now. I cannot omit mention of the famous wit and beauty, Miss Sally Carneal, niece of the original Nick Longworth, of Ohio, for, with her superb voice, she frequently entertained and entranced my father's guests. I recall one occasion when she sang, with inimitable pathos and wild passion, a song I never wish to hear again, "The Maniac." The little audience, roused to a pitch bordering on madness, was almost ready to shriek and tear its hair. Glendy Burke (does anybody remember him? He was an eligible *parti* then) fell in desperate love with her that night, and subsequently they married. All are gone now; and most of them forgotten, except, possibly, by an old lady, who sits at her fireside, and unfolds the book of memory. . . .

In course of time a Mme. Peuch took possession of the house on the St. Charles street corner, and, horrors! opened a boarding house, whereupon the aristocratic element gradually fluttered away. The Smiths and Labouisses went, as we thought, into the wilderness, up Carondelet Street to a kind of country place, with lots of ground and fig trees. The Buckners flew still further. I think they halted at Jackson Street—I am not sure the street had as yet a name. The Mathews moved to Annunciation Street. My father took his *lares et penates* to Canal

Street, and Mrs. Slocomb still further away, to Europe. The infection spread, and in a short time the whole "13 Buildings" pimpled out into cheap boarding houses or rented rooms. *Sic transit!* Where are all those fine people now? And what of the "13 Buildings"? Do they still stand and flaunt their signs over the places once adorned with immaculately shining brass name plates? or have they, in the march of events, also silently departed, and left places to be filled by a newer generation of buildings, in imitation of the lords of the earth that knew them and loved them and patronized them in their heyday?

XXIV

"OLD CREOLE DAYS" AND WAYS

IT was in the autumn of 1846 *La Belle Creole* carried me, a young girl, to Dr. Doussan's home, on the coast, above New Orleans. I was sent there to learn to speak French, which I had been fairly well taught to read and write. Both Dr. and Mme. Doussan were past middle life. The doctor was a native of France, madame a Creole, and the few *arpents* they owned were her inheritance. Their home was surrounded by a settlement of Creoles, pure and simple Creoles, such as I doubt exists to-day in the changed conditions that seventy years bring.

The simple natives, who had little patches, some of which amounted to little over an *arpent* (about an acre), were domiciled so conveniently near that it afforded an unending source of interest to a wide-awake American girl to see, listen to, and talk with them. They were not "poor folks" except possibly in the one meaning of the term. There was a family of Grandprés in that little settlement.

173

Hearing the name Grandpré would instantly call to mind the Grandprés of Louisiana's early days. Was not a Grandpré Governor, or Captain General, or something else as notable and commanding in Louisiana history, in the French, or more likely Spanish, occupancy of the country? This family descended from the original proud stock. The children, grown, half-grown, babies, at the time of which I write actually had a resident tutor, M. Marr, a man of no mean ability. I do not know how far they advanced in other branches of education, but their beautiful chirography would put to the blush any college graduate who hovers around our young girls to-day, and they signed themselves, too, with a grand flourish, De Grandpré. My old red and gilt album (every girl had an album and her friends wrote fulsome nonsense in it) has a *"Je suis très flatté, mademoiselle, de pouvoir m'inscrire,"* etc. signed L. De Grandpré. Looks as if I had flattered a nobleman of France! Doesn't it?

That flock of children of all ages and sizes were being educated well for their day and generation, albeit Grandpré *mère* strolled about in a gingham *blouse volante,* her frosty hair covered with a plaid *tignon;* and Grandpré *père* sniffled around (he had some catarrhal trouble, I guess) in carpet slippers. I do not think he ever did anything but bear the high-sounding name, and I never heard, after those album days, that the sons did either.

A family of Lafitons lived so near that we heard their parrot screaming for *"mon déjeuner"* every morning, long before it was time for anybody's breakfast. I think the bond of friendship that existed between *le vieux* Lafiton and Dr. Doussan must have been that they came from the same province in France. Most nights, Sundays as well, *"mon voisin,"* as the doctor called him, came for a game at cards. Long after my supper was served on a tray, and I was safely tucked into bed, madame presided at a banquet of gumbo, *jumbalaya* and salad, with their beloved Bordeaux, which was spread for the old gentlemen. Lafiton had straggling locks of white hair, falling over the collar of his great coat, reminding me of the picture of Little Nell's grandfather, and the home of the Lafitons carried out the simile, for it was as melancholy and cheerless as any "Old Curiosity Shop" could be. There were two bright, capable girls in it, though, who never knew or saw anything better than the rickety old house, way up on stilts, that they lived in. There they stitched and darned and mended and patched all day (Creole women are not lazy), and managed to make a creditable appearance for an afternoon promenade on the levee.

The two grown sons caught driftwood and fish, and when they tired of that exertion made crawfish nets. (*En parenthèse,* when I had a fifteenth birthday, Pete, the long-legged one, gave me a finger ring he had made of the tooth of a shell comb.) They did not own a skiff, much less a horse or *voiture.* For ever so long I thought Mme. Lafiton had chronic toothache, or some trouble in her jaws, for she always wore a handkerchief over her head, tied under the chin, and also a look of discomfort. In time I discovered that style of headdress, and that troubled smile, were peculiarly her own, and did not signify anything in particular.

We had other neighbors less picturesque than those I have mentioned. Madame had a cousin living quite near, who had, as had all Creole women in those days, a great flock of children. The Dubroca family seemed to be fairly well-to-do. Mr. Dubroca was sugar-maker for a nearby planter. Madame and her daughter Alzire were thrifty, hospitable and kindly. The sons, as they grew up, were sent to schools and colleges. Madame was a sister of Mrs. (Judge) Eustis of New Orleans, both being daughters of Valèrie Allain, a planter of means, whose property when divided among his children did not amount to much for each.

That brings me to the Favrot family. Judge

Favrot was a prominent citizen of the parish, and his son, a law student when I knew him, was much above the average. I scarce should mention this family that I saw almost daily and knew so well in connection with the obscure Creoles of the simpler life that I met and knew quite as intimately. The judge, and his son, were violinists. It was no unusual thing for him to play dance music for us, accommodating old gentleman that he was! We always had to adjourn to Lafiton's to "trip the light fantastic," for there was a great barn of a room, with bare floor, and no furniture to mention, which they called *le salon*.

Mme. Doussan often visited friends, by rowboat, on the opposite side of the river. She felt the responsibility of the care of the young girls, so strangely placed in her hands, so she never embarked on her frequent visits by boat or *voiture* without the company of one she might have esteemed an incumbrance if I had not already been received into the holy of holies of her loving heart.

There were two families of Choppins we saw frequently. The daughter of one, quite a child then, became at a later date wife of Dauphin. The eldest son of the other Choppin family, a youth of less than twenty, was already studying medicine in the office of a country town doctor. We saw much of him, the bright, attractive fellow! as he used to row himself over to the impromptu dances in the Lafiton salon. Later his ambition carried him to Paris, and later still he returned, a distinguished physician and surgeon, to New Orleans. He was a devoted citizen also. None who heard his impassioned address, and his rendering in thrilling tones the inspiring *"Aux Armes! Citoyens"* of the Marseillaise from the steps of Clay's monument, on Canal street, at the beginning of the war, ever forgot it.

Madame and I often visited other families in Baton Rouge, the Bonnecazes, Lanoues, Huguets and so on. As I remember, all lived over or in the rear of their shops. Very many families lived over shops in those days, not always over their own shops either. John Winthrop, a scion of the Massachusetts John Winthrop, and his aristocratic family lived over Symes' lace store, on Royal street in New Orleans. There was a shoemaker's establishment on the ground floor of the Miltenberger residence. My father's family lived over an exchange broker's office on Canal Street. In 1842, when a mob raided, or threatened to raid, banks and exchange brokers' offices, the strong box of the firm in our basement was conveyed to my mother for safekeeping. But this was in New Orleans, and I see I am wandering from my Creole friends on the coast, where I delighted to visit with *ma chère madame.*

Twice during that lovely six months' episode of my life, escorted by the doctor, we boarded the fascinating *Belle Creole* and made longer flights and longer visits to relatives of madame living beyond a voiture's possibilities. Once it was to spend a few days with the Valcour Aimes at their incomparable home; at another time we had two never-to-be-forgotten days at Sosthène Allain's, where I met two sweet girls of my own age. Then and there began a friendship that continued through our young ladyhood. We were three inseparable companions until three weddings sent us (as is the nature of things) on divergent paths. Celeste went to Paris, so remote then that she was practically lost to us. I do not suppose a single one of those who made those six months of my girlhood so happy is living to-day. Some have left no descendants; I do not know who has or who has not, but I pay this tribute to the Creole simple life, that seems in the retrospect almost ideal, and no episode of my checkered life is sweeter to recall.

Dr. Doussan was a botanist. His garden was the mecca of all lovers of plant life. I imagine it was excelled only by the noted grounds of the Valcour Aimes. Fruit and vegetables were sent daily in a skiff to the town market. *Ma chère madame,* in her black silk *blouse volante* and her cap, with stiff, fluted frill tied under the chin, often let me help her make the formal little bouquets for the market, the dear old stiff bouquets, flat as a plate and nestling in a frill of lace paper! The doctor spent hours in his cabinet with his botanical treasures. Daily I was summoned to read to him his *Paris Journal,* and to write a composition. No teacher could have been more painstaking; no scholar more appreciative.

Early in 1847 a nephew of the doctor's arrived from France, a dapper, Frenchified youth of eighteen. The Doussans were childless, but they had adopted a young girl. At the time of which I write she was about my age, and was being educated at Sacré Cœur Convent. She was home only for Easter vacation. No one told me, no one even hinted it, but I intuitively understood that a *mariage de convenance* was planned for the dapper young Frenchman and the pretty blonde girl, and the visit was meant to introduce Marie to her *prétendu;* they seemed to accept the arrangement complacently, but I was most interested in watching the proceedings, and, to say the least, much entertained.

It was fully fifty years after these events when

Doussan *neveu* and I met again, two old gray-haired folks. When the first frost of astonishment melted, and we could recognize each other, we had a grand time recalling places and people. How we laughed over the remembrance of the antics of the doctor's pet monkey; and, oh yes! the voluble Lafiton parrot! For a brief hour we lived again the halcyon days of fifteen and eighteen. The following year Doussan passed away—severing for me the last living link that bound me to the simple Creole life, on the borders of which I had such a happy girlhood.

XXV

A VISIT TO VALCOUR AIME PLANTATION

*L*A BELLE CREOLE! That name will bring a smile, mayhap a tear, to your grandmother, so many sweet reminiscences of her young girlhood may be associated with the little coast packet that carried her a-visiting from New Orleans to plantation homes in "the days that were," those leisurely days when there were no rail cars tearing and crashing over the land, no express companies to forward packages, no common carriers of any sort. A boat like *La Belle Creole* was a necessity. On her trips she stopped at every little town and country post office, like Brusle landing and Lobdell's store; answered every signal and every hail, shuttling across the river, back and forth, touching here for a keg of *sirop de batterie,* a hamper of oranges; touching at the very next plantation to take in somebody's carpetbag or put ashore somebody's darky, Capt. Ure always at his post on deck to expedite every move. *La Belle Creole* was not a freight boat, but a passenger packet, par excellence. There were boats galore to handle freight, but only one *Belle Creole!* "Steamboat ahoy!" We slow up, a gentleman rushes down from his plantation house, followed by a darky, carpetbag in hand. A plank is quickly run out, touching the shore, steadied by deckhands; passenger rushes aboard, has a handshake with Capt. Ure, and away we go to perhaps another hail. In the cabin the scene is like that of an "afternoon tea," an "at home," a "reception," whatever you will, for everybody knows everybody, and everybody shakes hands with everybody, and thus the newcomer is welcomed to the social atmosphere of a circle of Creole friends. *"Comment ca va?"* *"Aye! quel chance! c'est toi,"* are heard on every side, for some of these people rarely meet except in transit. And so, we sail along; the simple little craft is glorified by the magnetic influence of its passengers.

M. Champomier is on board. Everybody knows *le vieux* Champomier. He mingles with all, conspicuously carries his memorandum book and pencil, and we all know he is "on business bent," getting from any and every available source statistics of the year's crop of sugar. Whether he acted for a corporation, or it was his individual enterprise, I never knew, but he visited the planters, traveled up and down and all around the sugar region, and in the spring compiled and computed and published in a small, paper-covered book (price $5) the name and address of every planter and the amount of sugar made on each individual estate. "Champomier's report" was considered as authentic as need be for the planter to know what his neighbor's crop actually amounted to, and the city merchant to adjust his mortgages and loans on a safe basis.

It was after midnight when the plank was thrown out to touch the levee of the Valcour Aime plantation; midnight in late March, 1847. Deckhands steadied the wabbling plank till three persons and their little baggage were safely landed ashore. A tram (as it is called to-day) was awaiting the doctor, Tante Lise and myself, then a girl of fifteen. Darkies with torches preceded and followed us to the house, not so far away, only a short walk, but Tante Lise must not be permitted to walk at that hour of the night. The tram was nothing more than a flat car, fitted for the occasion with seats, on a short railroad leading to the sugar refinery, which I believe was the first in the state. A dusky housekeeper received us at the house. Not knowing at what hour we might appear, the family had retired. *Belle Creole,* as may be supposed, had no fixed schedule of arrivals or departures. Fires were already alight in our rooms, affording a cheery welcome. Before we were ready for bed basins of hot water were brought for the inevitable foot bath of the Creole. Something warm to drink, a *tisane* probably—I remember I thought it might be ambrosia, fit for the gods, it was so deliciously refreshing. Then I was tenderly tucked into bed, and told to *"dormez bien,"* which I straightway proceeded to do.

The sun was already proclaiming a bright spring day when I inhaled the odor, and opened my eyes to a full-blown rose on my pillow; and gracious, how good! a steaming cup of *café au lait*. On our descent to the breakfast room we received an effusive and cordial greeting from M. and Mme. Valcour, and their daughter Félicie, a girl of my own age. The air was redolent of the delicious odor of roses, the windows open to the floor upon the garden, the floor of the room not one step higher than the garden walks. The Valcour Aime house was a two-story structure. The long, main building faced, of course, the roadway and the river; there was a long L at each end, running back, thus forming three sides of a square court. A broad and partly jalousied balcony extended entirely around the three sides of the building, fronting the court. This balcony afforded the entrances to a seemingly endless series of living and sleeping rooms, the whole house being, so to say, one room deep only. The first floor, flush with the ground, was entirely paved with square blocks of stone or brick. There were to be found the small and the grand dining rooms, the master's office and den and the various and sundry domestic departments. The salon opened on the second floor balcony. The paved court below was protected by the deep balconies and an awning. The assemblage of all the family and the favorite resort of their multitudinous guests, madame's basket, mademoiselle's embroidery frame, the box of cigars, the comfortable lounging chairs, were to be found in that entrancing court.

M. Valcour, tall and graceful, was at that time in the prime of life, and was my (romantic) ideal of a French marquis; Mme. Valcour, inclined to *embonpoint* and vivacious, kissed me and called me *"ma petite,"* though I was quite her height. But the charm of my visit to that incomparable mansion, the like of which is not to be found on the Mississippi River to-day, was the daughter, Félicie, who at once took me under her wing and entertained me as only a well-bred young girl can. She showed me all over the premises, opening door after door, that I could see how adequate the accommodations for the guests who frequently filled the house; into the salon that I might see and listen to the chimes of the gilt clock Gabie had sent from Paris. Gabriel Aime, the only son, was then in Europe. Sweet Félicie never tired of talking of Gabie and showing me the pretty trifles from abroad (so far away then) he had sent home from time to time. She sent for the key, and opened the door of Gabie's room, that I might see how he had left it, and, "Mamma won't have a thing changed; she wants him to find his gun and boots and cap just where he left them." Girl-like, she confided to me that she would be a young lady when Gabie came, and they would have a house in the city and a box at the opera, for Gabie loved music.

By this time a number of the Roman family arrived. M. Valcour's oldest daughter had married Gov. Roman's son, and a flock of Roman grandchildren came with their parents to welcome the doctor and Tante Lise, and incidentally the young girl with them. The Valcours and Romans were closely related, independent of the marriage of their children. Both families being related to Tante Lise also, there was a great reunion and rejoicing when the tante made her annual visit. The governess, a New England woman, was accorded a holiday, in which Félicie participated. Years after, perhaps as many as forty years, I met and renewed acquaintance with that governess in her New England town. Only recently she passed away, having outlived, I understand, all the little pupils who clustered around "Dear Miss Goddard."

Félicie and I, with a whole escort of followers, explored the spacious grounds, considered the finest in Louisiana. There was a miniature river, meandering in and out and around the beautifully kept parterres, the tiny banks of which were an unbroken mass of blooming violets. A long-legged man might have been able to step across this tiny stream, but it was spanned at intervals by bridges of various designs, some rustic, some stone, but all furnished with parapets, so one would not tumble in and drown, as a little Roman remarked. If it had not been before Perry's expedition to Japan, at any rate before his report was printed and circulated, one might have supposed M. Valcour received his inspiration in landscape gardening from the queer little Eastern people. There were summer houses draped with strange, foreign-looking vines; a pagoda on a mound, the entrance of which was reached by a flight of steps. It was an octagonal building, with stained-glass windows, and it struck my inexperienced eye as a very wonderful and surprising bit of architecture. Further on was—a mountain! covered from base to top with beds of blooming violets. A narrow, winding path led to the summit, from which a comprehensive view was obtained of the extensive grounds, bounded by a series of conservatories. It was enchanting. There I saw for the first time the magnolia frascati, at that date a real rarity.

Another day, doctor, Tante Lise, Félicie and I were rowed in a skiff across the river to Sacré Coeur Convent to see tante's adopted daughter, Marie. I recall spending the day there, the kindly nuns showing the little heretic all through the building, and being rowed back to the plantation at sunset.

Next morning the *Belle Creole* was due, and our visit to fairyland was drawing to a close. The call, *"la Vapeur,"* rushed us to the landing in the tram, the "whole pack in full cry" of the Roman children running by the side and calling adieu to dear Tante Lise. We gingerly walked the plank, in single file. The boat backed out to get her leeway, and once more for a moment we were in full view of the house. Two figures fluttered handkerchiefs from the balcony, Mme. Valcour and Félicie waving a last adieu—alas! a last. On entering the cabin, behold the ubiquitous M. Champomier, with his everlasting book and pencil. As he greeted the doctor I heard (in French, of course), "Can you tell me the exact amount of——?" I fled, and at the rear end of the boat I had one more last glimpse of Valcour Aime's plantation. Alas! the last.

A month later I was on a clipper ship, the *Silas Holmes,* bound for a New England school. That Yankee, *Silas Holmes,* was a transport during the war, and like many a war relic has long been out of commission, if not out of existence. And the dainty *Belle Creole,* gone too! like thousands of Belles Creoles of her day and date.

Dear Félicie married Alfred Roman, adding another link of relationship to the Roman and Valcour Aime families, and the adored and only son, Gabriel Aime, died (I think Tante Lise wrote me) abroad.

I should like to know. No, I do not want to know. I already know too many wrecked homes and vanished fortunes and broken hearts. I want always to think of the Valcour Aime home and its charming hospitality, as I saw it and knew it, and loved it more than sixty years ago, when I waved a last adieu—alas! a last.

XXVI

THE OLD PLANTATION LIFE

IT is almost a half century since the old plantation days. Only those who number threescore years and ten have a personal remembrance of the cares, duties and pleasures of the old
plantation life. Only those who bore the cares, discharged the duties and prepared the way for the
pleasures really understand the life that died and
was buried fifty years ago. People who know so
much about that fanatic John Brown and the fantastic "Uncle Tom's Cabin" are asking what one
fought and bled for (did he bleed?) and what the
other was written for. Some of those inquiring
souls are over fifty years old, and what is more,
their fathers were slave owners. The few of us
tottering around who can tell of the old plantation
life are threescore years and ten, and if we do not
hasten to tell the story it may never be told. It is
well to leave a record of a life that has passed beyond resurrection, a glorified record it may appear,
for as we stand beside the bier of a loved and life-

long friend, we recall only his virtues. So as I look back on the old plantation life only the comforts and pleasures troop before me. It had its duties, but they were not onerous; its cares, but they were not burdensome, nor were its pleasures excessive. What we planned and accomplished for our slaves afforded us more satisfaction than any man of the present day can feel for his grand stables of hunters and roadsters and racers, that absorb his time and means. . . .

Booker Washington, in that very interesting volume, "Up from Slavery," tells of his early life when his mother (he never knew his father, and thinks he was a white man) was the slave of a well-to-do Virginia farmer, and the slave quarters had dirt floors. That may have been in the clay hills of Virginia, but I never saw a cabin, unless it was a pig pen, with a dirt floor. I am no apologist for slavery; the whites suffered more from its demoralizing influence than the blacks, but we were born to it, grew up with it, lived with it, and it was our daily life. We did well by it; no people could have done better. It is past now. When I tell of my own home it is to tell of the plantation homes of everybody I knew. We did not differ or vary to any extent in our modes of life and management.

Slaves were comfortably housed. Their cabins

ARLINGTON PLANTATION ON THE MISSISSIPPI

were elevated above the ground, two rooms in each building, a chimney between, a porch in front and windows on two sides. The slaves were well fed and well clothed in osnaburgs and linseys cut and made in the sewing room of the "big house." Though the hook worm theory was not at that time exploited they were well shod. There were drones; I guess there were hook worms too, but we did not know it. The old and infirm had light tasks. Men pottered around the woodpile, or tended the cows on their promenades over the levee, and the women sewed a little and quarreled, as idly disposed old folks will, among themselves (we who visit almshouses now know how that is) or fussed with the frolicking children. I never saw in those days a negro with spectacles, or one who seemed to need them.

There was an infirmary for the sick, and a day nursery for the babies, under the charge of a granny, a well-ventilated room with a spacious fireplace, where pots and kettles were always on hand, mush and herb teas always on tap; there the babies were deposited in cribs all day while the mothers were at work in the fields. No woman went to work until her child was a month old. A large diary folio record was kept by the overseer of all the incidents of the plantation; when a woman was confined, when she was sent again to the field, who was ill in the hospital, if doctor was summoned, what part of the canefield was being cultivated day by day, when sugar-making began, when finished, what the yield of the various "cuts," how many hogsheads and barrels of molasses shipped and by what boats; all these items and ever so many more were recorded. A doctor was employed at $600 per annum. He came only in extreme cases. Headaches and stomach aches, earaches, toothaches and backaches, all these minor ills came under the care of the overseer and "Gunn's Domestic Medicine," a formidable volume of instruction. The lady, the "mistis" of the big house, made frequent visits to the quarter lot, saw that things were kept tidy and ministered to the sick.

We did not have "made-over" dishes, cold meats nor stale bread on our tables; little darkies were sent by the half sick and aged for "left overs." Children were not bottlefed or spoonfed; they consumed pot liquor and mush and molasses as soon as they were weaned. Corn, cowpeas and turnips were cultivated for the slaves, and when there was an overplus of garden vegetables it was sent to the quarter kitchen. Their meat was pickled pork—it was called "clear sides"—shipped from Kentucky or Missouri. All their cooking was done by two cooks in a big kitchen, but every cabin had a fireplace, with a pot or skillet, of course, for we all know how the darky dotes on little messes of her own doing. All the doors had locks, and the women went to the field with the key hung around their necks.

Each spring at house-cleaning, cabins were white-washed inside and out; also the stables and other plantation buildings, the fences and trees as high up as a long pole or brush could reach. From Saturday noon till Monday was holiday, when the enterprising men chopped wood, for which they were paid, and the drones sunned themselves on the porch steps, and the women washed their clothes. I knew of only one planter who made his negroes work on Sundays. He was an Englishman who married into a plantation. The indignant neighbors called the attention of the grand jury in that case, with success, too. During sugar-making everybody worked day and night, but the season was short, terminating in December.

I cannot recall more than three deaths in ten years. I have no record to refer to (I guess that plantation folio afforded some information to the Union army). There was a burial ground for the slaves. One of them, the engineer, by the way, and a mighty good negro, too, acted as preacher. He married and buried and in all ways ministered to the spiritual needs of his flock. I recall teaching Lewis to sing "Canaan." He wanted to learn a hymn, and had a lusty bass voice, while I did not have any at all. Lewis was not the only accomplished negro. We did not have white labor. There were slave carpenters, coopers, masons and sugar makers; women who cut and made all clothing, shirts, coats, pantaloons, dresses.

By law no child under ten years of age could be sold from its mother. I suppose that law is obsolete now! It happened a negro child born in the penitentiary of a convict mother, named Alroy, had to remain ten years in confinement; he was taught reading and writing, probably all the Rs, by the convicts, while he imbibed in such surroundings a good many less desirable accomplishments. Hon. Mr. Alroy represented his native parish in the Louisiana Legislature of reconstruction times. He was better fitted probably than some of his dusky colleagues, for he could read the laws; some of them could not. That is also of the dead past, thank God, and has no bearing on the old plantation life, except as an illustration of the law regarding slaves.

The "big house" had no fastenings on the front and back doors. In the absence of my husband one time I was awakened, in the dead hour of night, by

a touch on my shoulder. "It's me, mistis; de levee's broke." A crevasse! Without taking time
to put on an extra gown, I was an hour giving orders
and dispatching men to the planters, even twenty
miles off, for assistance.

For a week thereafter, day and night, I fairly
lived on horseback at the levee, superintending the
repair work in place of my absent husband and our
inefficient overseer. Each planter affected by the
crevasse came, or sent an overseer with a force of
slaves, who worked in hour shifts, to their waists
in the water, driving piles and heaping sand bags.
As the shifts changed the men were given a dram
and hot soup or coffee, and sent to a huge bonfire
nearby to dry themselves.

Another time I landed from a boat at the witch-
ing hour between midnight and dawn. The boat's
bell and whistle sounded to attract some light
sleeper. By the time I was fairly ashore a glim-
mering light of a lantern was seen. I was escorted
to the house by the coachman, but if any other
negro had responded I should have felt quite as
safe.

Mammy Charlotte was supreme in the domestic
department. The little cupbearers from the quarters reported to her for the "dreenings" of the coffee pot or the left-over soup. The visitor by the

library fire called to her for a glass of wine or a "finger" of whisky. I called Charlotte to ask what we were going to have for dinner. She was the busy one, and every plantation had just such a mammy. Charlotte and I belonged to the same church. When there was a vacant seat in the carriage Sunday morning she was called to occupy it.

One of our neighbors, that a New Englander would call a "near" man, owned a few acres adjoining ours, but too remote from his plantation to be advantageously cultivated. He would not fence his property nor work his road, nor keep his levee in repair (it was just there we had the crevasse); however, it afforded good pasturage for Uncle Billy's cow, and for us, a supply of mushrooms. Billy's nets and lines supplied us with shrimp and fish, small catfish that William cooked *à la pompano*, not a poor imitation of that delectable Gulf dainty. I heard Charlotte berating Billy for not bringing in some more of those fine shrimp, when he knew, too, there was company in the house. Imagine my consternation at Billy's reply, "Dey done gorn; dat ole drowned mule is floated away."

Col. Hicky was our nearest neighbor, on Hope estate. When the dear old man was eighty and I was twenty-five we were great chums. He never passed in his buggy if I was visible on the lawn or porch without stopping for a chat. There was frequent interchange of neighborly courtesies. He had fine large pecans, and we didn't; we had celery and he didn't, so there was much flitting back and forth of baskets. If we were having an unusual occasion, like the dinner my husband gave in honor of Messrs. Slidell and Benjamin, when they were elected to the United States Senate, a big basket came from Hope estate. Didn't the dear old gentleman send a capon turkey which was too big for any dish we had, and didn't we have to borrow the Hicky dish?

Col. Hicky had a birthday dinner, when he was eighty-two, and a grand dinner it was, to be sure. Sam Moore—I never knew just who he was, or why he was so essential at every function—sat at the host's right. The Colonel was too deaf to hear all the *bon mots,* and Sam interpreted for him, and read in a loud voice all the toasts, some of which were very original and bright. Anyone remembering Col. Winthrop, or better still, Judge Avery, can understand there was no lack of wit and sparkle in any toast they might make.

XXVII

PEOPLE I HAVE ENTERTAINED

I IMAGINE all of us have read "People I Have Smiled With," or, "People I Have Known," but not many are writing about "People I Have Entertained." Rocking away the remnant of a long and varied life, I find myself dreamingly entertaining guests who are long since departed to the "House of Many Mansions," guests who came and stayed, and went, some of whom I had never seen before, and some I never heard from after, but there are guests and guests, as every housewife knows. Particularly country house guests come, whose city houses are not open to what a neighbor of mine calls "trunk visitors." In the days of which I write, every house, especially every plantation house, had a conspicuous latch string outside the door. I amuse my grandchildren with tales of the varied assortment of visitors I had "befo' de war," just as I had conjured to rest their mothers and fathers when they clamored to be told again about the gentleman who brought his own sheets and coffee pot, or the lady who wanted to pray all the time. I feel I am telling these tales for the last time. They don't point a moral, for no guest can do to-day, nor will hereafter, the things some of my guests did, let us think, in the innocence of their hearts.

The first visitor I recall when I was a bride in my new home, was a distinguished, eccentric, literary man, a bachelor, and a Creole, brim full of cranks and kinks, but a delightful conversationalist withal. Before he arrived I knew he was coming from a visit to an adjacent parish where his great heart had been touched by the witchery of a young girl. With his Sancho, the Don Quixote had been storming the citadel, and to continue the simile he struck a windmill, and so was put to flight. Now he was accepting my husband's invitation to rest, and salve his wounds at our home. I was amazed when my housemaid told me he had not only brought his valet, but his own linen sheets and his coffee pot! I understood then why he was not an acceptable suitor. Linen sheets and the coffee pot would scare any prospective housewife. When I knew what a blunder he had committed, I confess to little sympathy in his discomfort. That old gentleman died full of honors and deeply lamented, in New Orleans, a few years ago.

Mrs. Breckinridge was our guest, while her husband was vice-president. The presidential candidates, almost forgotten now, were Buchanan and Breckinridge. She was active and eager to have her husband mount to the top of the ladder of preferment, and did no little engineering in his behalf that winter. Mrs. Breckinridge was charming, a delightful visitor, a relative by marriage to us, but so remote, that if she had not been so lovely and the vice-president so distinguished, the dim connection would never have been thought of. Her aspirations were not realized, and he was tail to another presidential kite, that could not be made to fly. We did not meet Mrs. Breckinridge after that long visit, and the last time I saw her husband he was a fleeing Confederate general in Havana, without incumbrance of any kind, so he was not our "trunk visitor."

During the early fifties a planter from Bayou Lafourche bought a plantation on the Mississippi River, fully five miles from us, and on the opposite side of the river, as well. My husband, in his grandiloquent flamboyant manner, invited him to bring his family to our house to stay till their *lares et penates* were settled in their new home. The man, in the same grandiloquent, flamboyant style, accepted. When I asked how many there were in the family, my hospitable husband replied that he only heard mention of a wife. In due time a little Lafourche packet, with ever so much turning and backing, blowing of whistle and ringing of bells, as if to announce a surprise (which it certainly did), ran out a plank at our levee, and a whole procession walked that plank and filed up the path to the house. I looked from an upper window, and counted the guests as they marched up, in twos and threes: A man and his wife, her aged mother and brother, four boys, ranging from three to ten years, and a darky with the baby in arms!

One guest room had been made ready, but three additional chambers were at once put in commission. By the time wraps had been removed and fresh fires made all over the house—it was midwinter—I was ten times more breathless than my unexpected crowd. Every day for over a week the man and his wife were conveyed to their new home in our carriage, and there they stayed from morn to dewy eve. The aged grandmother was left in my special care. She was unable to cope with the untrained boys, as, indeed, all of us were. The uncle had rheumatism or something that confined him to his bed most of the time. So the boys were left to their own devices, to gallop in and out of doors, from the muddy garden to the Brussels carpets, all hours of the day. The baby squalled, and the nurse spanked it, and I didn't care.

One stormy day the boys found occupation indoors that was very diverting. They extracted every button from a tufted, upholstered chair in the library, the one their grandmother most affected, and with hairpin and nail, scratched hieroglyphics all over a newly-painted mantel, till it looked like it had been taken from some buried city of Egypt. Thank goodness! Visits don't last forever. In the course of time the family moved into the new home, and gave a house-warming ball within the next week—*vive la bagatelle!*

Reading with great interest a newly published book, "The Circuit Rider's Wife," brings vividly to mind a visitor we once had. She was one of the sweetest and loveliest of women. She was a Methodist, the only one in a wide acquaintance I ever met, who claimed to have "the gift of sanctification." I do not believe one possesses the power within oneself to resist sin, nor do I mean to inject religious views and doctrines in these remarks about "People I Have Entertained," but I do say, if there ever was a really sanctified woman it was this Mrs. Abe Smith of Mississippi. She was our guest one short, happy, glorified week. She read her Bible chapter to us every morning, and prayed with and for us all day long, if we wanted, and we generally did, for surely she had the gift of prayer. I never listened to such uplifting prayers as dear Mrs. Smith could utter; her very voice was an inspiration. She was highly connected and highly cultivated and had a vocal training that comprised very intricate music, but with "The Coming of the Lord" she confined her voice entirely to psalms and hymns. Her mission was to pray and sing, but no doubt when the harvest was waiting, in some meeting house, she could exhort with an eloquence equal to the most earnest itinerant in the pulpit. We had one strange glorification and sanctification, but it was interrupted by the coming of a Methodist preacher, who claimed to having sought, in vain, the gift of sanctification. The last few days of lovely Sister Smith's visit were spent in the library with closed doors, wrestling with the halting soul of Brother Camp.

These were the expiring days of the old "Peace which passeth understanding." After that came the war, which sorely tried the heart of the glorified woman, and she proved faithful to her gift of sanctification even unto the bitter end. . . .

One November day I entered my library with an open letter of introduction in my hand, to say to the young man, placidly warming himself at the fire, that the letter was not meant for my husband, who

was not at home, but for his brother. He replied
he understood the brother was not in Louisiana, and
he took the liberty of transferring the introductory
epistle to the next of kin. He was a young doctor,
threatened with lung trouble, who had come South
to spend some time in somebody's sugar house. I
frankly told him that our sugar house was not by
any means a suitable place for an invalid, but (I
glanced out of the door and saw his vehicle had departed and his trunk was on the porch) I would be
pleased to have him remain my guest until my husband returned to see what could be devised to further the invalid's plan. Northern and Western
people, who never had been in a sugar house and inhaled the warm fumes of boiling cane juice, night
and day, and incidentally submitted to the discomforts of an open building, not intended for sleeping
quarters, thought that the treatment, as they chose
to call it, was a cure for tuberculosis. My guest
found himself quite comfortable, and remained in
our home five months. Nothing more was said
about sugar house treatment. By spring, like
a butterfly, he emerged into the sunlight, strong
and well and ready to fly to pastures new,
which he did. We did not even hear from that
doctor again. He was a physician in good practice in Galveston during the war, and told

Gen. Magruder he thought he had met us years before!

Every planter in my day entertained strangers who came and went, like a dream. Some were grateful for their entertainment, some did not so much as write "bread and butter" notes, after their departure.

Queer, inquisitive folks lighted upon us now and then. I recall a party of Philadelphians who arrived at the adjacent town with a note of introduction to the president of the bank. They said they wanted to visit a plantation and see the working thereof. That hospitable husband of mine happened to be passing; he was called in and introduced to the party, and he invited them for the whole of the next day. They came, they saw, I don't know if they thought they conquered. We thought so, for they were on a tour of observation. They were delightfully informal and interesting people. We accompanied them to the canefield—the negroes happened to be at work quite near the house—into some of the cabins, the infirmary, where they were surprised to find not one inmate, into the nursery where the babies were sleeping in cribs, and the older children eating mush and molasses. They had to taste the food, had to talk to the granny about her babies, had to ask after her health. Meeting a negro man, walking as brisk as anybody, with a hoe over his shoulder, they had to inquire as to his condition, and must have been surprised to hear what an awful misery he had in his back. They had to see where the plantation sewing, and the cooking, were done. I began to think before it was all over we were superintendents of some penal institution and were enduring a visit from the committee of inspection. However, they were very attractive, naïve visitors, surprised at everything. After luncheon, waited upon by a negro boy on a broad grin— it was all so very funny to him—they took their departure, and my husband and I had a merry laugh over the incidents of the day. It was rather an interesting interlude in our quiet life, and remoteness from the abolition storm that was hovering over the land.

All the people I entertained were not queer. We had a house full always of gay, young people, young girls from the North that were my schoolmates in New Haven, girls who were my playmates, and the friends of my young ladyhood in New Orleans, fresh, bright, happy girls, who rode horseback, sang and danced and made merry all through the house. All are gone now. Only the sweet memory of them comes to me in my solitary day-dreams.

XXVIII

A MONUMENT TO MAMMIES

LET us have a memorial, before the last of us who had a black mammy passes away. We who still linger would love to see a granite monument to the memory of the dear mammy who fostered our childhood. Our grandchildren, indeed our children, will never know the kind of mammies their ancestors were blessed with.

I know of two only of the old stock of nurses and housekeepers left. They were grown women when Sherman marched through Georgia, destroying their old homes, laying waste the land, and Butler sat down in New Orleans, wreaking vengeance on their hapless masters, and scattering their little bands of servants to the four winds. These two mammies I wot of remained with their own white folks. The Georgia one lived in a family I visited, a faithful old woman, doing her utmost to fill a gap (and gaps were of constant occurrence) in any branch of household duty. Mammy was a supernumerary after the children grew up, but when the new-fangled housemaid swept her trailing skirts out of the premises, mammy filled her place till another of that same half-educated sort came. When cook flared up and refused to do her duty in the way to which she was called, mammy descended into the deserted kitchen.

One day I overheard the son of that family, who was about to start to a Northern college, say: "Mammy, put on your Sunday black silk; I want you to go down the street with me; I am going to have your picture taken." "What fur, son?" "I want it with the rest of my family to put on my bureau at college." "Lord! son, you ought'en to hav' my black face to show to dem Yankees; den you'll tell 'em I'se your mammy." However, the pleased old darky, as black as her Sunday silk, had her picture taken just like "son" wanted. I have a copy of it now. God bless her!

A family from the extreme South comes every summer to a quiet place in Connecticut and brings mammy to take care of the little ones. I doubt if they feel they could come without her. Mammy is pure black; no adulterated blood under that skin —black, flat-nosed and homely, but the children adore her, and she "makes them mind, too," she proudly tells you. Every boarder in that big house knows mammy, but I doubt if one of them knows her name; I do not. It warms my heart to shake hands with those two remnants of a dear past civilization, the only two I ever met.

When a child I made frequent visits to my cousin, Judge Chinn's plantation, in West Baton Rouge. I believe that hospitable house has long since vanished into the river, with its store of pleasant memories. How I always, when I arrived there, had to run find mammy first thing, and how she folded me in her warm embrace and delighted my ears with, "How dis chile do grow." Every visitor at that grand, hospitable home knew mammy. She always stood back of the judge's chair, and with signals directed the young girls how to wait at table. She managed after the children grew up, married and settled (some of them settled, Creole fashion, in the home nest too) that whole big and mixed household, where another generation of babies came to claim a portion of her love and care. Nobody thought to go to the judge or his wife for anything. "All applications," to use an office phrase, "made to mammy." She was always ready to point the way or to help one through it.

Casually meeting Mrs. Chinn and inquiring of the various members of her family that from long absence I had lost sight of, "And mammy," I said. The dear old lady burst into tears. Mammy had died holding the hand of the sorrowing mistress, her last words, "My work is done. I tried to do my best," and God knows she did.

We had a mammy in my mother's house when I was a wee little thing, and we children loved her right along all the week till Saturday night, when the ponderous woman brought the big washtub upstairs and two pails of hot water. We hated mammy then, for she had a heavy hand and a searching eye, and a rough wash rag full of soapsuds. Not a fold in the ear, nor a crease in the plump body escaped her vigilance. I really think we were glad when we outgrew need of her assistance at those dreaded Saturday night's baths, and she went to other little lambs, in pastures new.

When I went a bride to my husband's home, Charlotte, his old mammy, met us and proudly escorted us within doors, where were fresh flowers and a blazing fire (it was long past midnight, and dreadfully stormy too), and every comfort prepared and ready for "the coming of the bride." I felt then and there mammy would be a comfort for me and a real help, and so she proved, in all my sunny life in the plantation home and in the dark days of the war, too. My Mammy Charlotte had complete charge of everything about the house. She had been thoroughly trained by my husband's mother. She made the jellies and the pickles, the ice cream, the cakes, doing a little of everything to make our home comfortable and happy. And often she remarked that no one in the house did more and had less to show for it at night than she did. That is a truth about many households, one does all the neglected things, and picks up all the loose threads. Guests were made to understand if they required anything, from a riding horse to a fresh stick on the fire, from a mint julep to a bedroom candle, they had only to call Charlotte. She was never beyond the reach of a summons, day or night. She was mammy to all the children of the house, and all the other children that floated in from other people's houses. It was Mammy Charlotte who hurriedly secreted the spoons (!) when a Federal cavalry company came prancing down the road toward our gates. It was mammy who ran to my bedside to whisper, "Don't you get skeered, they does look like gentlemen;" and after they had taken a drink of water and trotted off again it was mammy back to say, "It's all right; they didn't say nothin' 'bout spoons." Even at that early date and that remote spot from Butler's headquarters the matter of spoons had been so freely and laughingly discussed that the sable crowd of witnesses that surrounded every household must have taken the idea that collecting spoons was "the chief end of man."

I pity the little ones of to-day with no black mammy of their very own to cuddle them to her warm bosom and comfort them, and tell them funny rhymes about "The Monkey and the Baboon's Sister," to make them forget their griefs in a merry laugh. The high-falutin' nurses they have now, here to-day, gone to-morrow, without any anchorage in our hearts and homes, are not and never could be made mammies like we of threescore years and ten were blessed with.

Who of us that lived within a day's journey of Col. Hicky but remembers his Milly, the mammy of that grand, big household? The dear Colonel lived to see great-grandchildren grow up, and Milly mammied at least three generations at "Hope Estate." She was a famous nurse. Mind you, this was decades before trained nurses arrived on the stage. How many of us remember how tenderly and untiringly Milly nursed some of our invalids to health! Her services were tendered, and oh! how gratefully accepted. With a sad heart I recall a sick baby I nursed until Milly came and put me to bed and took the ailing child in her tender arms. For two days and nights unto the end she watched the little flickering spark.

A MONUMENT TO MAMMIES

When Mr. Sidell removed his family to Washington after his election to the United States Senate, I traveled in their company several days. The children had their colored mammy to care for them. She had been raised in the Deslonde family, a trusted servant. I was struck with the system and care with which she managed her little charges from Mathilde, a girl in her teens, down to baby Johnny. She lived with them during those troublous times in Washington, she accompanied the family to Paris, and I presume died there. Always dressed in a neat calico gown, a fichu and *tignon,* even in Paris she did not alter her dress nor wear another headgear than her own bandana. There's a mammy to immortalize!

Then let us raise a monument to the mammies of the days that were. Quickly, too, before the last one of us who were crowned with such a blessing shall have passed away " 'mid the shadows that flee in the night."

XXIX

MARY ANN AND MARTHA ANN

THE story of Mary Ann and Martha Ann and the red bonnet has been so often retold to my children and grandchildren that every detail has been retained, and in its completeness as I give it here, it is a bit of authentic family history "dressed up" as its hearers love it.

"What kin we do, Ma'y Ann? I dun hear Miss Liza talkin' 'bout it agin, and 'lowin' it got to be found." The two little negroes sat under a widespreading pecan tree that scattered its shade and its late autumn nuts over the grassy lawn of a spacious Southern mansion. They crouched closely together, heads touching, voices whispering and faces turned to the river road, their scanty linsey skirts drawn tightly over little black legs, so that no searching eye from the broad veranda could spy them. Mary Ann looked anxiously around, and, drawing her knotty, kinky head closer still to Martha's softer locks, whispered: "Marm Charlotte gwine to clean out de L, and you know she'll go in dat room fust thing."

216

Marthy sprang back with dilated eyes.

"Ma'y Ann, it carnt stay dar; it's gotten to cum outen dar, oh Lordy! What did you put it dar in the fust place fur?"

"I didn't put it dar." Ma'y Ann's eyes flashed. "You fotch it dar your own self, unner your apern; you sed it was yourn and Miss Ellen giv it to you."

Marthy sprang to her feet. "Miss Ellen never giv me nothin' in her whole life." She shook her clenched fist in Ma'y Ann's face, then burst into tears. The stolen conference, like many another that had preceded it, was opened in a spirit of mutual conciliation, but as the interview progressed and interest waxed, the poor little negroes became fierce in their alarm, fast losing sight of the turpitude of the deed committed in common in the overmastering anxiety of each one to shift the entire blame on the other.

"Hush, gal, set down; I hear Marm Charlotte dis bery minit; she mustn't kotch me under dis here pecon tree agin. I was down here yisterday, tryin' to dig a hole where we's settin' now! I want ter berry de rotten thing. Marm Charlotte kotch'd me here, and she ax'd what I doin' and I 'low'd I was gitten pecons fur de turkeys, and she 'sponded she low'd ter tell me when to feed de turkeys."

Marthy Ann slowly resumed her seat, taking care

to get well behind the pecan tree. She was nervously sobbing, "She's kept me—a—lookin' fur it —till I feared to go in—our—room—feared to find it—a settin' on de baid—Oh, Ma'y Ann, what made you take hit?"

Ma'y Ann's eyes flashed fire. She was of the heroic sort, and by no wise melted by Marthy's lamentations and tears.

"I didn't take hit; you tuck hit, and you know you did; you's de biggest rascal on de place. You does a thing, den you goes whinin' and cryin' 'bout hit. I does a thing, I jist 'sponds fur hit and sticks hit out."

Marthy wiped her eyes on the linsey skirt and tried to imbibe some of her companion's courage.

"Well, Ma'y Ann, you put it whar tis and ghostes cum out ev'ry night and ties me wid de long, red strings."

"No ghostes cum arter me," said Ma'y Ann, bridling up. "Dat shows you put it dar your own self."

"We ain't got no time ter talk and fuss; we got ter find a place to put hit now. God knows it cums atter me ev'y night, and las' night de debbel had it on, Ma'y Ann. I seed him; he jist strutted all around de room wid it on his haid and de ribbons was tied to his horns."

"Oh, Lordy, Marthy, is he got hit now?" The terrified child sprang to her feet and gazed distractedly up the tree. "Marthy, we kin fling hit up in dis tree; won't de debbil let hit stay in de crotch?"

The strained eyes eagerly searched for a sheltering limb that would catch and conceal the thing, the ghost of which would not lay, day or night. Marm Charlotte had never relaxed in her search, in bureaus, and armchairs, behind hanging dresses, in the big cedar chest, among the blankets, upon top shelves, in old bandboxes, in trunks, over bed testers, downstairs in china closets, among plates and dishes, under parlor sofas and over library bookcases. Ma'y Ann and Marthy Ann had no rest. They made believe to search the garden, after the house had been pulled to pieces, going down among the artichoke bushes and the cherokee rose hedge that smothered the orchard fence, wishing and praying somebody might find it in one of those impossible places all torn by squirrels or made into nests by birds.

. . . .

Christmas, with its turkeys and capons fattened on pecan nuts, its dances and flirtations in the wide halls of the big house, its weddings and breakdowns in the negro quarters, had come and gone. The

whirr of the ponderous mill had ceased; the towering
chimney of the sugar house no longer waved its
plume of smoke by day nor scattered its showers of
sparks by night. Busy spiders spun nets over big,
dusty kettles, and hung filmy veils from the tall
rafters. Keen-eyed mice scampered over the floors
and scuffled in the walls of the deserted building
whence the last hogshead of sugar and barrel of
molasses had been removed, and the key turned in
the great door of the sugar house. Tiny spears of
cane were sprouting up all over the newly plowed
fields. Drain and ditches were bubbling over, and
young crawfish darting back and forth in their sparkling waters. The balmy air of early summer,
freighted with odors of honeysuckle and cape
jessamine, and melodious with the whistle and
trill of mocking birds, floated into the open
windows and doors of the plantation dwelling.
The shadowy crepe myrtle tree scattered crimpy
pink blossoms over the lawn. Lady Banks
rose vines festooned the trellises and scram-
bled in wild confusion over the roof of the
well house, waving its golden radiance in the
soft, sunny air. Cherokee and Chickasaw hedges,
with prodigal luxuriance, covered the rough
wooden fences, holding multitudes of pink and
white blossoms in thorny embrace, and sheltering

the secret nests of roaming turkey hens and their wild-eyed broods.

"Well, Levi, you'se dun your job, and it wus a big one, too."

"Yes, William, I whitewashed as much as ten miles o' fencing, and all de trees in de stable lot, besides de cabins and de chicken houses."

"Ten miles o' fencing," replied William doubtfully. "I didn't 'low dere wuz dat much on de whole plantation. Why, dey call hit ten miles from here to Manchac, and 'bout ten from here to Cohite."

"I mean ten miles in and out; about five miles one side de fence and five miles de odder."

"Oh! that-a-way," said William dubiously. "Charlotte, give Mr. Stucker another dodger."

The speakers were two negro men, one in the shirt sleeves and long apron that betokened the household cook, the other in the shiny, shabby "store clothes" of the town darky. They sat at the kitchen table, in front of a window commanding a view of newly whitewashed fences and trees. Etiquette required that William should play the role of host, on this, the last morning of the whitewasher's stay. Charlotte had laid the cloth and placed the plates and knives for two, and served the fried bacon and hot corn dodgers to Mr. Levi Stucker, a free man, who had a house of his own and a wife to wait on him and in view of this dignity and state was deemed entitled to unusual consideration.

"Lemme ask you, Charlotte," said Stucker, carefully splitting his dodger, and sopping the hot crumbs in the bacon gravy, "is you missed ary thing outen de yard on dese premises? Caze I heard dem two little gals havin' a big talk in dat room next to me last night; you knows dat's a mighty weaky boardin' 'tween dose rooms and a pusson don't have to listen to hear. I bin hearin' 'em movin' 'bout and a whisperin' most ginerally every night when dey ought most likely to be asleep. Las' night a old owl was a squinchin' on dat mulberry tree by de winder, and de shutter hit slammed. Dat woke dem gals up; it was atter midnight; dey was skeert, one on 'em begin to blubber and sed de debbil was dar to kotch 'em. From de way dey talked— (but it was mystifyin', I tell you)—I 'lowed in my mind dem gals had stole somethin', I couldn't gather what, fur dey didn't name no specials, but sure's you born dey's up to somethin', and skeered to death 'bout its bein' foun' out."

Charlotte stopped on her way to the frying pan with widening eyes and uplifted fork, and listened attentively, with an occasional jerk of the head toward William.

"Jist tell me," pursued Levi, "if you 'low dose

gals to have de run of de quarters, caze dey gits mischief in dere heads if dey run wid quarter niggers."

"No, sir," responded the woman emphatically, "dey never goes down dar; I'm keerful 'bout dat— onreason'ble keerful; no, sir, if I was to let 'em have the run o' dat quarter lot dere would never be a cold biskit nor a cup o' clabber in dis house de minit atter you put 'em outen your hands. No, sir, Mr. Stucker, if old Hannah, or ary of de sick niggers down dar wants anything from dis house dey got to send one of their own little niggers wid de cup or de pan, and I pintedly gives 'em what's needed; dere's nuff work for Ma'y Ann and Marthy Ann 'bout dis house 'dout dey visitin' at de quarters and waitin' on quarter niggers. I bet, dough, dey's bin in some mischief I ain't had time to ferret out."

After a pause she continued, "And you say you think dey done stole somethin'?"

"Yes," answered Stucker, pushing back his chair and rising from the table; "yes, I understand somethin' of dat natur', if you has missed ary thing."

"We did miss dat currycomb what William comb his har wid; it was a bran new, kinder stiff one, and he missed it last Sunday," replied Charlotte."

"Dat jist fallen outen de winder, it warn't lost,"

223

interrupted William, who had been watching for a favorable opportunity to join the conversation.

"Yes, dem spawns foun' hit outdoors, when I tole 'em I'd skin 'em if it wasn't perjuced," said Charlotte, turning to William, who thereupon relapsed into acquiescent silence.

"It warn't no currycomb dey was talkin' 'bout last night," said Stucker, jerking first one leg then the other to free his shaggy breeches of dodger crumbs.

"Jist hold on a minit," said Charlotte, stepping to the kitchen door and shouting, "Ma'y Ann and Marthy Ann, whar's you?"

"Here I is, ma'am, I's comin', yes 'em," was responded from an upper porch, and the two little darkies scuffled down the back stairs.

"Jist you two run down to de orchard whar I kin see you all de time, hear me? All de time, and look fur dat Dominiker hen's nest. I hear her cacklin' down dar, and don't neither of you dar' cum back till you find it. If you cum back 'fore I call you, I'll pickle you well. Run!"

Two little guinea blue cotton skirts whisked through a gap in the rose hedge and emerged in the deep grass of the orchard, before Charlotte turned back into the kitchen, satisfied they were at a distance, and still under her observation. Levi

Stucker meanwhile, having carefully tied his two weeks' earnings in the corner of his red cotton hand-kerchief, and shared his last "chaw" of tobacco with William, swung his bundle from the end of his long whitewash pole and departed, with the shambling, shuffling gait of the typical Southern negro.

"I'm gwine upstairs, William, and I'll ramshackle dat room till I find out what's dar," said the woman. She slowly mounted the stairs, down which the two culprits had so lately descended with flying feet, and turned into a small room on the servants' gallery. She glanced around the bare apartment the two little negroes called their own. There was a battered trunk against the wall with a damaged cover and no fastening of any kind, a rickety chair and a bed. Charlotte tore the linsey dresses, home-spun petticoats and check aprons from nails behind the door, shaking and critically examining each article. In the trunk she found remnants of rag dolls and broken toys and bits of quilt pieces that had been their playthings for time out of mind. There were no pockets to examine, no locks to pry open. "Dey don't need no pockets to carry dere money in, and no locked up trunks fur dere jewelry," Charlotte always said. It was her habit to go in and out their room freely, to see that it was kept in some kind of order and the bed regularly made up. The door of the room was always open, and no means afforded for securing it on the inside. Notwithstanding these precautions of Charlotte, who practically accepted the doctrine of infant depravity, there was a mystery concealed in that room that at intervals almost throttled the two little negroes, and, strange to say, with all the woman's vigilance, had slumbered months within sound of her voice. She rapidly threw the clothes on the window sill, turned the trunk inside out and pushed its battered frame into the middle of the floor.

Nothing now remained to be searched but the plain unpainted bed. It was neatly made up, the coarse brown blankets securely tucked in all around. Charlotte whisked that off and dragged after it the cotton mattress which rested on a "sack bottom," secured by interlacing cords to the bed frame. There was revealed the hidden secret! Crushed quite flat and sticking to the sacking, long under pressure of the cotton mattress and the tossing and tumbling children, what trick of dainty beauty lay before her? It was so crumpled and smothered, torn and ragged, soiled with fleeces of cotton lint that had sifted through the bed seams, and covered with dust and grime that but for glimpses of its original form and color here and there it would never have been recognized. Charlotte snatched it

226

out and fled to the porch to see if Ma'y Ann and
Marthy Ann were still down in the orchard. There
they lay, prone in the soft grass, happy as only
children, and black ones at that, can be. Four little
ebony legs kicked up in the air, and the sound of
merry shouts reached Charlotte's ear.

"You'll fly dem laigs to sum purpose yit, fur
I lay I'll git Marse Jim to giv you a breakdown
dat'll make dem laigs tired," she said to herself.
"You jist lay dar," she muttered, as she descended
the steps. "You needn't waste your time (it's a
awful short one) lookin' for aigs dat de ole Dominiker ain't never laid yit."

.   .   .   .

The deep window of the library was wide open,
the sash thrown up and an easy lounging chair drawn
to the veranda, on which reposed the towering form
of the planter, lazily smoking a cigar, and looking
off upon the broad, swift river at a passing steamboat, floating so high on its swelling waves that its
deck was almost on a line with the top of the grass-
covered levee. Its passengers, thronging the
"guards" in the fragrance of a fine morning, seemed
almost near enough to the spectator on shore to
respond to a friendly nod of the head. The delicate
lady of the mansion sat silently within, also watching
the passing boat.

"I see some one waving a paper from the *Belle Creole*. I believe that's Green. Yes, he has tied a handkerchief to his crutch, and is waving that."

The planter rose as he spoke and stood for a moment for a better view. "Here, give me something, quick, to wave back at him."

At this critical moment Charlotte appeared on the scene. "This will do," he exclaimed, catching the velvet wreck from the astonished woman's grasp and tossing it aloft, holding it by the long strings.

"Lord! jist see Marse Jim wid dat bonnet I dun foun', dat you lost 'fore grinding time, Miss Liza, and whar you spec it was? Right onder Ma'y Ann's bed."

"My bonnet! for pity's sake, only look at it. Look!"

"It don't look much like a bonnet. It's more like a red rag to make the turkeys gobble," replied the master, disdainfully, throwing it to Charlotte.

"My bonnet I paid Olympe twenty dollars for, and never wore it but once; see the satin strings! And just look at the cape at the back! And the feather poppies!"

Charlotte straightened herself up, holding the crumpled bonnet and turning it around to show its proportions. It was of the "skyscraper" shape, made on stiff millinette, that is more easily broken

than bent. Mashed sideways, it showed in its flat-
tened state as much of the satin lining as of velvet
cover.

"Levi Stucker ain't no fool. He tole me and
William he heard Ma'y Ann and Marthy Ann whisperin' and plannin' in dere room nights till he was
sure dey was a hatchin' mischief, ef dey hadn't already hatched more snakes dan dey could kiver, so
I 'low'd I'd go and ramshackle dat room o' theirn,
and onder de baid, Marse Jim, 'twixt de sackin' and
de cotton baid, way onder de very middle, I found
dis bonnet what I bin lookin' fur ever since grindin'
time. Now, Marse Jim, dere ain't no use in talkin'
to dem gals; dere ain't no use in readin' no cater-
kism to 'em, nor in Miss Liza telling no more tales
to 'em 'bout dat liar Anifera, or sum sich name.
No use in whippin' 'em, nudder. If I'se whipped
dem two niggers once fur not lookin' fur dis bonnet
when I sont 'em to, I'se whipped 'em forty times.
Dat didn't make 'em find what they hid demselves,
and it ain't going to do 'em no good now. Marse
Jim, you jist got to skeer de very life outen 'em,
and send 'em to de canefields. Dey is rascals and
rogues."

"Well, Charlotte," he responded, "put the bonnet
on this side, out of sight, and bring those children
here. I'll see what I can do."

As Charlotte left he turned to his tender-hearted wife and told her, "It is important those little negroes should have a lesson that would be of some use. Charlotte is right on the subject of moral suasion as far as those little imps are concerned, so don't let your kindness and sympathy interfere with my conduct of the case. Keep in the background, and I will give them a lesson they will not soon forget."

"I can't imagine what could have induced those children to make way with that bonnet," said Miss Liza, meditatively, as she looked at the crumpled wreck on the floor.

"Perhaps mischief, perhaps accident. The thing is to make them acknowledge the theft. Entrenched as they are behind a whole barricade of lies and deceit, the thing is to make them capitulate," replied the husband.

"Cum right in; don't be modest now. Marse Jim sont fur you," was heard in Charlotte's bantering tone, as she appeared in the doorway, half-leading, half-dragging the reluctant culprits, who already began to sniff a coming battle. With some difficulty she marshaled them before the master and stood close at hand ready to offer moral support if the court of inquiry gave any signs of weakening, or to cut off retreat on the part of the little darkies if they became too alarmed to "stand fire."

"Well, Mary and Martha, where have you been?" inquired Marse Jim, in his blandest and most conciliatory tone.

"Down in de orchard lookin' for aigs fur Marm Charlotte." "And we was findin' some when she hollowed fur us to cum to de house." "De Dominicker hen got nest in de haige." "She's settin', too."

"Hold on, hold on, don't both of you talk at once. I didn't ask about the hen's nest. Have you been all over the orchard in the hot sun?"

"Yes, sir." "Yes, sir, we goes anywhar fur Marm Charlotte." "She sont us." "Yes, sir, she sont us fur aigs." "An' we was findin' sum too." "Dat Dominicker hen——"

With uplifted restraining hand he said: "Hush, don't both talk at once. Let me talk some. Did you go away down there without your bonnet?"

"We ain't got no bonnet." "Me and Ma'y Ann don't wear bonnets, Marse Jim."

"Yes, you have a bonnet. Isn't this your bonnet?" the master said, in his quiet, inquiring tone, holding up before their bulging eyes the dilapidated wreck that they had not dared look at in all the months they had buried it out of sight. Ma'y

Ann steadfastly turned her face away from the ghost. She bit her lips, but uttered not a word.

"No, Marse Jim—I—I—er, Marse Jim, I feel sick, sick," stammered Marthy, as she trembled so she almost fell.

"Sick! Give me your hand." She quickly recovered, and clasped the tawny paws behind her back. "Give me your hand; let me feel your pulse." Reluctantly she proffered the hand. "There, now," he said, letting the limp little hand fall to her side. "You feel chilly, don't you? Go sit down on that step." Marthy sidled slowly away, tears welling her eyes and her whole frame shaken with suppressed sobs.

"Stop dat cryin'; nobody ain't doin' nuthin' to you; stop dat foolishness and listen to what Marse Jim is a sayin' to you two onreasonable rapscallions," said Charlotte, in a severe tone. She held Mary Ann (who was making ready to fly at the first opportunity) by the back of her neckband.

"Let Martha alone, Charlotte, she is weakening; we'll talk about the bonnet to Mary Ann, she knows."

"No, Marse Jim, I 'clar I never see dat bonnet in all my life; I 'clar I never did. I 'clar——"

"Hush," said the master in a stern voice, "let

me ask a question or two, and only answer what I ask."

"Tell de truth, too," ejaculated Charlotte, "onless you want de debbil to kotch you."

"Give me your hand." The child clutched at her cotton skirt with both hands. He reached out, quietly and forcibly took one skinny little black paw in his firm grasp. Drawing the shrinking, reluctant child toward him, he fixed his eyes upon her averted face. "Now look me right in the eye; everybody does that to people who are talking to them; look me in the eye. What made you hide that bonnet? Look at me when I am talking to you."

"I didn't neber see dat bonnet b'fore. I 'clar——"

"Stop, look at me; don't look at Martha, she's better." The child's eyes dropped. "Don't look at the floor, look me in the eye."

"Marse Jim, slap her; make her look at you."

"Be quiet, Charlotte; she's going to tell, I want to help her," replied the imperturbable inquisitor in his blandest tones. Still holding the reluctant hand and drawing the figure more closely to him, he said, "You say you never saw this bonnet? How came it in your bed?"

There was a long pause. The little negro at last gathered herself up, and, with a gleam of inspiration, exclaimed: "Marse Jim, de rats put it dar—de rats runs all over dat floor nights. Me and Marthy Ann jist hears 'em jist toting things all around. Rats put it dar, Marse Jim, big rats."

"Dat's a lie," said Charlotte, positively. "Nary rat on dat floor. Marse Jim, you jist foolin' way your time on dese niggers."

The baffled master turned toward the crouching figure on the steps. She was still trembling, her face buried in her hands. He saw she was ready to confess, but he was determined Mary Ann should acknowledge also.

"Have you a mammy, Mary Ann?" he inquired.

"No, Marse Jim; I ain't got no mammy; I ain't never had no mammy, and my daddy, he's daid, and I ain't——"

"Hush, I didn't ask all that. If you haven't a mammy there's no one to care if you die. I am sure I don't want little girls round the house that steal and lie. Nobody else would have you; nobody would buy you, and I can't keep you here. It's come to a pretty pass when a lady can't lay her bonnet on the bed without you two little imps taking it and hiding it for months, and lying about it right straight along. You have no mammy to cry for you, and I don't want you, and Miss Liza don't want you. What can be done with you?"

Martha sobbed, on the veranda step, and Mary looked defiant, but no response came to that repeated inquiry. After a pause, Mary Ann bridled up; the matter in question seemed to be taking a broader range; the bonnet seemed to be merging in generalities, and might in time sink into the other question of what can be done with them. Martha's courage also revived, so she could respond to the inquiry of her parentage.

"I ain't neber had no daddy, and my mammy she's married to long Phil now."

The planter shifted his legs, looked abroad in a meditative way, then turned to the charge.

'Well, now, you girls want to tell us all you know about this," holding up again before them the battered brim and crushed poppies and long, dingy ribbons. Martha buried her face again, and Mary was suddenly interested in the gambols of a squirrel in the pecan tree. Neither culprit would look at the evidence of their guilt. "What will become of you? I can't keep you and nobody will buy a rogue; nobody wants you."

"My mammy wants me, Marse Jim," whimpered the scared Martha.

"No, your mother is Nancy, isn't she? She's a good woman and don't want a rogue and a liar tied to her all her days." Another long pause.

235

"Come here, Martha, both of you stand by Charlotte and hold her hands. I will give you one more chance. Which—one—of—you—stole—that bonnet? Did both of you do it together? Who hid it? What made you do it?" There was a pause between the questions, not one word of response. Martha's tears dropped on her little naked foot, while Mary Ann looked vacantly at the nimble squirrel in apparent indifference, not a muscle of her face giving any evidence of emotion.

"Marse Jim," said Charlotte, whose impatience increased as she saw signs of action on the part of the inquisitor. "Marse Jim, what you gwine to do? It's no use er whippin' dese gals; dere hides is like cowhide and whippin' ain't no good noways fur liars. Killin' is good for such."

The planter rose from his chair, straightened his tired limbs and kicked the bonnet out of his way. "Bring them along, Charlotte. I'll see what I can do."

Charlotte, with a firm grasp of each child, followed the tall leader, who, as he turned into the hall, tossed a nod and a significant wink to his wife. She obediently rose and followed. In all the interview the mistress had remained a passive but interested spectator, feeling sure that at a critical moment a signal from her husband would afford her an op-

portunity to intervene. The master led his followers
straight to the well-house, under whose vine-clad arbor reposed the dripping bucket, attached by a wind-
lass to an endless chain.

"I think it best to drown them," he quietly remarked. The little group filled the arbor. William
and Billy, the gardener; Delia, the laundress; Lucy,
the maid; Sawny, the "woodpile boy" and Oliver,
who "went wid de buggy," attracted by the spectacle,
gathered around the outskirts. The story of the finding of the long lost bonnet had spread over the
yard and premises; fragments had even wafted to
"the quarters," with the mysterious rapidity and
certainty that always attended a household event in
the old plantation days.

"Mary Ann first," said the master, as catching
her suddenly and firmly by the neckband of her
dress and imprisoning her struggling legs by wrap-
ping her skirts tightly around them, he held her over
the well-hole, head a little down. The struggles
and writhings of the child were of no avail in the
grasp of the strong man. "I want you to tell the
truth and promise never to tell another lie before
I drop you down this well." The child squirmed
and screamed in the relentless clutch, swearing entire ignorance of the whole matter. Charlotte felt
she must pile on the agony, so she saw "de debbil

down dar wid his pitchfork, ready to ketch her."
That vision was too much for the now thoroughly
alarmed little darky.

"I tuck it, Marse Jim, I tuck it," she screamed.

"Will you ever steal again?" still holding her
over the well, where in her own little reflection in
the placid water she was convinced to her dying
day she had seen "de debbil."

"Neber, neber, 'fore God, neber agin."

"Never tell another lie if I let you off?"

"Neber, Marse Jim; neber's long as I lib. Please
the Lord and Miss Liza, I'll be a good little nigger;
neber lie agin if you'll lemme off dis time."

While that harrowing scene was being enacted
with the most determined and refractory of the little witches, and the spectators on the outskirts were
convulsed with laughter—every one of them had
at one time or another been suspected of the theft—
Martha, the tearful, was on her knees, holding de-
spairingly to Miss Liza's skirts and imploring her
"Jist to save me dis time, I'll be good, I'll neber
tell anoder lie. I'se got a mammy dat will cry fur
me, and I don't want ter die. Oh! save me frum
de debbil," she screamed, when Charlotte's voice
proclaimed him at the bottom of the well. "Don't
let de debbil have your good little nigger."

Confessions and promises being obtained, Mary

Ann was placed upon her feet. Four little black legs flew down the backyard; two little guinea-blue skirts flipped over the cowyard fence and two little dusky spots vanished in the distance. William called after them to "clip it 'fore de debbil gits outen dat well." Charlotte held her sides with outbursts of laughter that had been held in painful restraint.

"De debbil done skeer 'em more en Marse Jim," Sawny remarked, as he shambled back to the wood-pile.

"I think, my dear," said the planter, linking his arm into that of his wife and returning to the library with her, "I think those children had a lesson that may last them all their lives. They had to be scared into a confession."

"I hated to see them badgered," she replied. "I dropped a few tears over Martha myself—perhaps," with a smile, "she thought I was scared too."

Charlotte came in and picked up the wreck. "Miss Liza, I'se goin' to take dis bonnet, jist as it is, all tousled up and mashed and I'm gwine to make Ma'y Ann war it one day and Marthy Ann de next clean till dey gits sick o' bonnets; dey shall war it till de chillen come home Sat-day. I 'spose dere'll be sum laffin' done when de chillen sees Ma'y Ann wid dat bonnet tied on her haid."

.   .   .   .

Another winter had come and gone, and June was again filling the old plantation with its intoxicating odors and delicious melody. The little room on the back porch was darkened by a heavy curtain at the only window. A table drawn up by the rough wooden bed, made gay by a patchwork quilt, held a few medicine bottles, a cup and spoon; also a tumbler of pink and white roses. The quiet mistress moved about noiselessly, occasionally putting her cool hand upon the brow of the little sick negro, or gently stroking the thin, black fingers that lay listlessly upon the bright coverlet.

"Miss Liza, whar Ma'y Ann?" The lady turned her face from the questioner. After a moment's hesitation she replied, cheerfully: "She's all right, Martha."

"Miss Liza, whar is she? Whar Ma'y Ann?"

"She's down by the quarters now," was the unsatisfactory response. The weary patient closed her eyes for a few moments, but it was evident that with the first consciousness, following a severe illness, the child's thoughts turned to her old companion.

"She ain't bin here sence I was tuk sick." After a pause, "I want ter talk to Ma'y Ann 'bout sumthin'."

MARY ANN AND MARTHA ANN

"Tell me," said the mistress, soothingly, "what it was you wanted to see Mary for."

Both the little negroes had been ill of scarlet fever. The children of the household had not been allowed for weeks to come home for their Saturday holidays. Martha fell ill first, and Mary was removed into the room formerly occupied by Levi Stucker, where she soon fell a victim to the disease. The mistress and Charlotte only were allowed to minister to the invalids. Mary, the robust one of the two, the more mischievous, the one apparently better equipped for a struggle with disease, succumbed, after a few days of delirium. The busy hands were stilled, the flying feet arrested, the voluble tongue silenced, at the touch of the Angel of Death. The little body was carried past the "quarters" and beyond, to the negroes' "burying ground," where it lay in peaceful shadows of the trees the romping children loved so well. Martha lingered long on the mysterious border, fitfully fighting an apparently hopeless battle, the more tenderly and faithfully nursed by Mammy Charlotte, as the warm-hearted, childless woman realized the frail tenure of life held by the little negro whom she had ruled in varying moods of sternness and tenderness, untempered with judgment. With the fretful peevishness of convalescence, the sick child whined repeated desires to know "Whar Ma'y Ann?"

"What is it you want to tell Mary Ann to-day, when she is not here? Can't you tell me?" said the patient watcher.

"I jist want ter see her; I'se gwine ter tell you 'bout dat bonnet, Miss Liza, and she ain't here, and I mout die; sometimes folkses dies of broke laigs, and my laigs is broke. I want Ma'y Ann ter know I ain't goin' outen dis world wid dat bonnet on my soul."

The mistress drew closer to the bedside, stroked and patted the attenuated hand in a soothing way to quiet and compose the restless invalid.

"Maybe it's jist as good Ma'y Ann ain't here, Miss Liza. I kin tell de tale better'n when she is here to jine in." After a pause, apparently to marshal her thoughts more clearly, the child proceeded: "Dat time Miss Ellen cum here, she tuk outen her trunk a red bonnet, and she sed she had two on 'em jist alike, dat her chillen had wore out, and she fotched 'em fur me and Ma'y Ann. I was in dar and seed de bonnet, and you tuk hit, don't you 'member, Miss Liza? You tuk hit and sed no, Ma'y Ann and me had no use fur bonnets, and you know'd two pore little white gals at your church dat didn't have none, and you was goin' ter give 'em to dem.

I went out and tole Ma'y Ann all 'bout hit, and she 'low'd if we had bonnets we cud go to church too. Well, we talked tergedder 'bout dose bonnets, and we plan we'd take 'em ennyhow, fust time we seed 'em. Well, one night Ma'y Ann runned right in here, in dat very door. I was in here den. I shet de door and stood against it, and onder her apern she had de bonnet. She didn't find only one, but she grabbed dat. I tole her dat was the bery one Miss Ellen took outen her trunk, and me and Ma'y Ann, we tried it on our haids, 'fore dat bery piece o' lookin' glass stickin' on de wall dere, and we 'greed ter watch till we kotch de udder one, so we hid it in dat trunk dar, behind you, Miss Liza, and ev'ry day we tried hit on. I want ter tell you all 'bout hit 'fore Ma'y Ann gits back frum de quarters. I dun know how long we kep' hit in dat trunk, ontil one day dere was a awful fuss, eberybody skeered up, lookin' fur your bonnet, dat was missin'. Me and Ma'y Ann was glad. We couldn't find one of our bonnets now your'n wuz gone, too."

"Didn't you know you had taken my bonnet?" said the mistress, who was at last seeing through the mystery.

"Jist let me tell you de whole thing, Miss Liza. I bin layin' here long time thinkin' de straight uv hit, so Ma'y Ann can't bodder me when I telled it

243

to you. Ma'y Ann is dat sondacious she most make you b'lieve anythin'. No, Miss Liza, we never thought dat till one day I hear Miss Ellen say how nice dem red bonnets she brung did look on de Quiggins gals at church. Den Marm Charlotte, she begun agin 'bout your bonnet bein' missed and she searchin' fur hit all de time, and I hear her tell Sawny it wuz red and had black flowers on hit. Me and Ma'y Ann took de bonnet outen de trunk dat night and dere wuz de black flowers, jist like she sed, den we know'd you had give Miss Ellen's bonnets to the Quigginses, and Ma'y Ann had stole your'n. We hefted dis baid and put de bonnet under hit, and, please Gord, Miss Liza, I neber seed dat bonnet agin till Marse Jim shuck hit at us dat day."

"Why didn't you come tell me what you had done, and why you had done it, when you first found it out?"

"Miss Liza, we was afeerd. Marm Charlotte kep' sayin' whoever had dat bonnet wud be hung, and de odder negroes talked back. Thank de Lord, dey never seed hit, so Ma'y Ann and me didn't dar let on."

"Didn't you expect it would be found out some day?"

"Yes'em, I 'spec we did."

XXX

WHEN LEXINGTON WON THE RACE

EVERY Kentucky woman loves a horse, and when Lexington was entered in the great State stake in 1854 a crowd of the *crème de la crème* of the Blue Grass country clamored to be present at the race. The St. Charles Hotel, then in the hands of those genial hosts, Messrs. Hall and Hildreth, was crowded for the event, beyond its capacity, for when that Kentucky contingent of women, unheralded and unexpected, swarmed into its broad parlor and halls, even the servants' quarters, so near the roof that the only light admitted was skylight, were put into requisition. There was enough Blue Grass blood in my family to compel a rush to the city, and we had a "sky parlor," right next to the one occupied by Gen. John H. Morgan (simply "John" then. He won his spurs and title a decade or so later) and his Kentucky wife. It took us "forever and a day" to mount the stairs to our roosts, and we were so tired when we arrived that we actually found the quarters acceptable.

All the Breckinridges, Wards, Flournoys, Johnsons and Hunts in Kentucky were more or less financially interested in the superb racer. Those who did not own one drop of Lexington's blood, nor one hair of his tail, "put their money" on the horse, and therewith a financial interest was created. Every man, it seemed, in the place, that could spare the time, wanted to see the great race. "Lee Count," as a good many Kentuckians call Le Comte, was the most prominent rival of their boasted and beloved Lexington, and he showed mettle that astonished even those blind partisans, and added zest to the wagers. Ladies had never been in evidence at a horse race in Louisiana. The bare idea was a shock to the Creole mind, that dominated and controlled all the fashionable, indeed, all the respectable, minds in New Orleans at that day. But the Kentucky belles had minds of their own. Every mortal one of them felt a personal interest, and a personal pride, and a personal ambition in that Kentucky horse, though probably not ten out of the scores who rushed to see him race had ever seen him before, and when he did appear on the paddock he had to be pointed out to those enthusiastic admirers.

What a host of dashing, high-bred, blue-blooded Kentucky women swarmed the parlors, halls, rotunda of that, the finest hotel in all the land! How they talked, in the soft, Southern accent, so peculiarly their own! How they laughed! How they moved about, seemingly knowing everybody they met. How they bet! Gloves, fans, money, too, on their horse, when they found any one in all the crowd that was not a "Lexington horse" man. Those bright women dominated everything in their enthusiasm. I recall a host of them.

There was a lamentable scarcity of conveyances. Those Kentucky people who had never felt the lack of vehicles and horses, had apparently made small provision for travel to the course, so at the moment of departure, when a large party was almost driven to despair, Messrs. Hall and Hildreth ordered out the hotel stage, which was one of the "nine-passenger" type. A nine-passenger coach, one of the kind that was in vogue in the days of Pickwick, afforded seats inside for nine persons, and could accommodate as many outside as chose to pile on. The celerity with which those Kentucky women filled that coach and the Kentucky men covered the top was a sight worth seeing. No doubt when that stage rattled and bumped over the cobblestones, en route to Metaire, many a cautious Creole mamma made her innocent mam'zelles repair to the backyard while she hastily closed the shutters. It was like a circus van, though no circus had ever paraded those decorous streets.

Richard Tenbroeck (also a Kentuckian), who was associated in the management of the course, was on hand to receive the merry crowd from his own State, furnish it with grandstand seats and make it welcome in every way. According to my recollection the Kentucky women were the only females present, so very unfashionable it was for ladies to go to races in the extreme South. There may have been some *demi-mondaines* scattered here and there, in inconspicuous places.

The race, the only one I had ever witnessed, was tremendously exciting, and as the gallant horses swept round the last lap, Lexington, ever so little, in the lead, the uproar became quite deafening. One of the Johnson women, beautiful and enthusiastic, sprang upon the bench and said to her equally excited escort, "Hold me while I holler." He threw his strong arms about her and steadied her feet. "Now, holler"—and never did I hear the full compass of the female voice before, nor since. Such excitement, as we all know, is contagious, and it continued for days after the great achievement that put dear old Lexington in the front rank, and filled the pocketbooks of his owners, abettors and admirers.

WHEN LEXINGTON WON THE RACE

Of course, this race was practically an all-day venture, and, equally of course, people got hungry; and throats, most particularly Kentucky throats, awfully dry. Mr. Tenbroeck provided liberally for such a contingency, so a luncheon was served al fresco, with lots of champagne, which latter did not dampen the ardor of those terribly dry throats. We assembled in little groups around the viands, and there were jokes and puns and stories that varied the monotony of horse talk, that had dominated every other topic for days. In all the circles there was fun and frolic. Kentuckians can be very hilarious. The unique vehicle that carried our party back to the hotel rocked and tumbled tipsily along. The sprightly crowd that departed in a somewhat steady condition in the forenoon were sleepily tired when they gained their sky parlors later in the day. A brief rest must have revived them, for as we passed through the hall to a rather late breakfast the following morning, trays of empty glasses and bottles, flanked by freshly blacked boots and shoes, afforded evidence that more refreshments had been absorbed later, and the parties had returned to the Land of Nod.

XXXI

LOUISIANA STATE FAIR FIFTY YEARS AGO

IT was in 1859 or 1860—I cannot fix the exact dates of many events immediately prior to the war, for the rush of an overwhelming waste carried dates, as everything else, away, but it was before the war that several enterprising and advanced citizens of Louisiana planned and organized and "resolved" themselves into a committee to stimulate the indolent agricultural population to a more active life, by inaugurating a series of State agricultural and mechanical exhibitions, patterned as near as might be on the annual State and county fairs of Kentucky, Missouri and other enterprising agricultural States. Mr. John A. Dougherty, Major Sam Hart, George W. Ward, John Perkins, my husband, Mr. James McHatton and his brother Charles, Wm. A. Pike and others whose names escape me now, secured from the United States government, through the joint efforts of Hon. John Slidell and J. P. Benjamin, United States Senators from Louisiana, and Thomas Green Davidson, Representative of the Sixth District, temporary use of the then practically abandoned Barracks in Baton Rouge, as being the most available site in the State for the purpose of an experimental fair. Only a corporal's guard had been stationed there, to furl and unfurl the flag and to fire the evening gun, as evidence that the grounds were United States property. In those precincts and under those auspices, were held the first and the last and only "Louisiana State Agricultural and Mechanical Fair."

There came from New Orleans many exhibitors of farming implements and products; from plantations, whose owners happened to be "wide awake," cattle, horses, sugar, molasses, and all such; from the small farmer who occasionally read the papers, and thereby kept in touch with the march of events, pigs and poultry; and from the homes of enterprising women, all sorts of fancy work and domestic articles. There were quite handsome prizes of silver, worth competing for, offered by the managers. The parade ground was ample to "show off" harness horses. An area was fenced off for cattle, and side-show places assigned for pigs and poultry. The Barrack buildings, two stories in height, surrounding the enclosure, offered abundant room for the exhibit of farming utensils, harness, etc. Rooms were appropriated for

251

the luncheons and lounging places of friends and guests.

The first two days were rather disappointing, so few people understood just what was being attempted, but the number of the exhibitors increased day by day, so that, before the final day, the managers had reason to be enthusiastic at the success and consequent promise for future State fairs.

Old Mr. Kleinpeter, of the high lands, entered a sow with a litter of nine pigs, whereupon Granville Pierce "went one better" with a sow and fourteen pigs. To be sure, the pigs varied in size, and people made merry over the pig exhibit! From the "Cottage" plantation (Cottage, by the way, was a tremendous big house) came a hogshead of prize open kettle brown sugar. Immediately "Whitehall" plantation saw it could beat that—and next day a hogshead of the "Whitehall" brand was entered. It was thus the project expanded to creditable dimensions. An enterprising lady who had won a silver spoon prize at a similar fair in the West, entered a dressy bonnet, made entirely of fine corn shucks; bows, flowers, feathers and all! Whereupon, a smart miss from Grosse Tête sent three home-made sun bonnets. The domestic exhibit thus resolved itself into a competitive show. A Jew in town had met with indifferent success in a sewing machine venture (sewing machines were in their immaturity then, and not coveted by women who had domestics to order), till the happy thought of a chance at the fair. Soon there was a sewing machine on exhibition—a "Finkle and Lyon"—I don't forget the make, now happily out of existence, for in an evil moment, moved by the Jew's persuasive eloquence, I invested in a "Finkle and Lyon" which I quickly found could only be made to "run" by copious drenchings of olive oil, aided by the warm rays of the sun!

All the citizens of Baton Rouge entertained guests for the fair week, the Harney House and other small hostelries being totally inadequate. Several New Orleans merchants showed great interest in the venture. Cuthbert Slocomb entered a fine exhibit of plows, hoes and other farming tools, that were in his line of trade. So, also, did the firm of Slark, Day and Stauffer; Henderson & Gaines sent of their stock, as also did many others whose business brought them in contact with the agricultural world. The cattle display was quite surprisingly good, as were also the harness horses. The inexperienced judges of such stock were often criticised for their decisions, but the people were amiable and in a mood to enjoy everything.

Such an outpouring from the "Cajin" settlements

on the river, and on Bayou Tête and Bayou Fordoche, and such other communities of small preten-
sions, and still smaller achievements, never, I am
sure, had invaded Baton Rouge before. It was as
"good as a play" to watch their interest and enthusiasm, to see the greetings of families and friends,
who lived beyond the reach of a ramshackle *voiture*
and a worn-out horse. I do not recall the season of
the year that immortal fair occurred, but it must have
been in late winter, for I remember a small dish of
radishes on my lunch table, such a rarity that Col.
Sparks ate every one. How one does recall, after
a lapse of years, such insignificant things! Some of
the *bon vivants,* like Dr. French, Mr. Bonnecage,
and Dr. Harney, regretted that the enterprise was
not postponed till artichokes and river shrimp were
in season.

It seems almost immediately after that I accompanied my delegate husband to that ill-starred Demo-
cratic convention in Charleston, and almost the next
day that the Hon. J. P. Benjamin made his soul-
stirring speech in Congress, that magnificent burst
of impassioned oratory, whose prediction was never
verified; almost the next day that Hon. John Slidell
returned to Louisiana a sad, despondent man, and
old Tom Green Davidson hobbled back to Baton
Rouge on his crutches, so full of bitterness and hate

LOUISIANA STATE FAIR FIFTY YEARS AGO

—almost the next day that the flag that waved so gloriously over the parade ground where the hopes and aspirations of those enterprising citizens took flight, was hauled down.——

And after that—the Deluge!

XXXII

THE LAST CHRISTMAS

CHRISTMAS before the war. There never will be another in any land, with any peoples, like the Christmas of 1859—on the old plantation. Days beforehand preparations were in progress for the wedding at the quarters, and the ball at the "big house." Children coming home for the holidays were both amused and delighted to learn that Nancy Brackenridge was to be the quarter bride. "Nancy a bride! Oh, la!" they exclaimed. "Why Nancy must be forty years old." And she was going to marry Aleck, who, if he would wait a year or two, might marry Nancy's daughter. While the young schoolgirls were busy "letting out" the white satin ball dress that had descended from the parlor dance to the quarter bride, and were picking out and freshening up the wreath and corsage bouquet of lilies of the valley that had been the wedding flowers of the mistress of the big house, and while the boys were ransacking the distant woods for holly branches and magnolia boughs, enough for the ballroom as well as the wedding supper table, the family were busy with the multitudinous preparations for the annual dance, for which Arlington, with its ample parlors and halls, and its proverbial hospitality, was noted far and wide.

The children made molasses gingerbread and sweet potato pies, and one big bride's cake, with a real ring in it. They spread the table in the big quarters nursery, and the boys decorated it with greenery and a lot of cut paper fly catchers, laid on the roast mutton and pig, and hot biscuits from the big house kitchen, and the pies and cakes of the girls' own make. The girls proceeded to dress Nancy Brackenridge, pulling together that refractory satin waist which, though it had been "let out" to its fullest extent, still showed a sad gap, to be concealed by a dextrous arrangement of some discarded hair ribbons. Nancy was black as a crow and had rather a startling look in that dazzling white satin dress and the pure white flowers pinned to her kinks. At length the girls gave a finishing pat to the toilet, and their brothers pronounced her "bully," and called Marthy Ann to see how fine her mammy was.

As was the custom, the whole household went to the quarters to witness the wedding. Lewis, the plantation preacher, in a cast-off swallow-tail coat of Marse Jim's that was uncomfortably tight, especially about the waist line, performed the ceremony. Then my husband advanced and made some remarks, to the effect that this marriage was a solemn tie, and there must be no shirking of its duties; they must behave and be faithful to each other; he would have no foolishness. These remarks, though by no means elegant, fitted the occasion to a fraction. There were no high flights of eloquence which the darky mind could not reach, it was plain, unvarnished admonition.

The following morning, Christmas Day, the field negroes were summoned to the back porch of the big house, where Marse Jim, after a few preliminary remarks, distributed the presents—a head handkerchief, a pocketknife, a pipe, a dress for the baby, shoes for the growing boy (his first pair, maybe), etc., etc., down the list. Each gift was received with a "Thankee, sir," and, perhaps, also a remark anent its usefulness. Then after Charlotte brought forth the jug of whisky and the tin cups, and everyone had a comforting dram, they filed off to the quarters, with a week of holiday before them and a trip to town to do their little buying.

The very last Christmas on the old plantation

JAMES ALEXANDER McHATTON

we had a tree. None of us had ever seen a Christmas tree; there were no cedars or pines, so we finally settled upon a tall althea bush, hung presents on it, for all the house servants, as well as for the family and a few guests. The tree had to be lighted up, so it was postponed till evening. The idea of the house servants having such a celebration quite upset the little negroes. I heard one remark, "All us house niggers is going to be hung on a tree." Before the dawn of another Christmas the negroes had become discontented, demoralized and scattered, freer than the whites, for the blacks recognized no responsibilities whatever. The family had abandoned the old plantation home. We could not stand the changed condition of things any longer, and the Federals had entered into possession and completed the ruin. Very likely some reminiscent darky told new-found friends, "All de house niggers was hung on a tree last Christmas." I have heard from Northern lips even more astonishing stories of maltreated slaves than a wholesale hanging.

Frequently before the holidays some of the negroes were questioned as to what they would like to have, and the planter would make notes and have the order filled in the city. That, I think, was the custom at Whitehall plantation. I was visiting there on one occasion when a woman told Judge Chinn she wanted a mourning veil. "A mourning veil!" he replied. "I thought you were going to marry Tom this Christmas?" "I is, marster, but you know Jim died last grinding, and I ain't never mourned none for Jim. I want to mourn some 'fore I marries ag'in." I did not remain to see, but I do not doubt she got the mourning veil and had the melancholy satisfaction of wearing it around the quarter lot a few days before she married Tom.

After the departure of our happy negroes, whose voices and laughter could be heard long after the yard gate was closed and they had vanished out of sight, we rushed around like wild to complete preparations for the coming ball guests. They began to arrive in the afternoon from down the coast and from the opposite side of the river. Miles and miles some of them drove in carriages, with champagne baskets, capital forerunners of the modern suit case, tied on behind, and, like as not, a dusky maid perched on top of it; poor thing, the carriage being full, she had to travel in that precarious way, holding on for dear life. Those old-time turtle-back vehicles had outside a small single seat for the coachman only. Parties came also in skiffs, with their champagne baskets and maids. Long before time for the guests from town to appear mammas and maids were busy in the bedrooms, dressing their young ladies for the occasion. Meanwhile the plantation musicians were assembling, two violins, a flute, a triangle, and a tambourine. A platform had been erected at one end of the rooms, with kitchen chairs and cuspidors, for their accommodation. Our own negroes furnished the dance music, but we borrowed Col. Hicky's Washington for the tambourine. He was more expert than any "end man" you ever saw. He kicked it and butted it and struck it with elbow and heel, and rattled it in perfect unison with the other instruments, making more noise, and being himself a more inspiring sight, than all the rest of the band put together. Col. Hicky always said it was the only thing Washington was fit for, and he kept the worthless negro simply because he was the image (in bronze) of Gen. Lafayette. Col. Hicky was an octogenarian, and had seen Gen. Lafayette, so he could not have been mistaken. When Washington flagged, a few drops of whisky was all he needed to refresh his energies.

The whirl of the dance waxed as the night waned. The tired paterfamiliases sat around the rooms, too true to their mission to retire for a little snooze. They were restored to consciousness at intervals by liberal cups of strong coffee. Black William, our first violin, called out the figures,

"Ladies to the right!" "Set to your partners!"—
and the young people whirled and swung around
in the giddy reel as though they would never have
such another opportunity to dance—as, indeed, many
of them never did. From the porch and lawn windows black faces gazed at the inspiring scene. They
never saw the like again, either.

Laughing, wide-awake girls and tired fathers and
mothers started homeward at the first blush of
dawn, when they could plainly see their way over
the roads. I started too early from a party the
year before, and the buggy I was in ran over a dust-
colored cow lying asleep in the road. The nodding
maid again perilously perched on top the champagne basket, and skiffs with similar freight plied
across the broad river as soon as there was sufficient light to enable them to dodge a passing steamboat.

The last ball was a noble success. We danced on
and on, never thinking this was to be our last dance
in the big house. Clouds were hovering all about
us the following Christmas. No one had the heart
to dance then. The negroes had already become
restless and discontented. After that the Deluge!
The big house long ago slid into the voracious Mississippi. The quarters where the wedding feast was
spread are fallen into ruins, the negroes scattered

or dead. The children, so happy and so busy then, are now old people—the only ones left to look on this imperfectly drawn picture with any personal interest. We lived, indeed, a life never to be lived again.

XXXIII

A WEDDING IN WAR TIME

"MARSE GREEN says cum right away; he's gwine to marry Miss Fanny to de Captain."

"When?"

"Soon's I kin git de preacher. I can't wait for you; I ain't got no preacher yit."

That was a summons I had one hot day in early summer, in war times. Yankees in New Orleans; gunboats almost hourly reported "jist 'round de p'int"; and we people distractedly hanging on the ragged edge of alarm and anxiety, did not pause to think how impossible it was for us to know what was happening "jist 'round de p'int," for all information about things beyond our physical eyesight was questionable. In the rush of uncertain and unlooked-for events, we could not plan any future, even one day ahead, so overwhelmed were we in mind and estate (not to mention body) with the strenuousness of the pitiful present.

I hastily changed my dress and was ready when my carriage was brought to the door. "Marse

Green" (I will not give the full name; everybody in his old district knows who I mean), was a lawyer, a politician, a man of family, while not a family man, and his little cottage home in town was presided over, the best they knew how, by his three daughters, the eldest of whom was scarcely out of her teens. The disturbed state of the country had compelled me to stay quietly as I could at my plantation home, and in the absorbing and frequent rumor of Yankees coming, no real town news and gossip sifted in. Thus I had not heard that Miss Fanny's fiancé, a wounded soldier, was at Marse Green's.

I was driven at a rapid pace up the road and through the restless, crowded street throngs to the home of these motherless girls, whose New England governess had returned North. I had long been their mother's dearest friend, and a refuge for her daughters in all their troubles and perplexities. We were completely cut off from any reliable information of the doings of the world, almost at our doors. Everybody knew New Orleans had fallen and Butler was treading the prostrate people with hoofs of iron, and also it was only a matter of time when his rule would reach our town only 130 miles off. As a matter of course, under such circumstances, we were alive to any startling rumor.

Marse Green, who did things by fits and starts, and did them very thoroughly, too, when he started, had announced to his daughters on the morning of my visit that they must be ready by early dawn the following day to move themselves and everything else they might need to his plantation on the Amite. Then the man of family shook the dust of further assistance from his feet and proceeded to his office for the day's enlightenments. Of course, all business of a legal nature was suspended. The few able-bodied men lingering outside the rank of fighters, who were facetiously called "Druthers," because they'd druther not fight, or in other words, would druther stay at home, had dropped in Marse Green's office to while pleasantly away their idle time. The old gentleman hobbled on his crutches to his favorite chair and was telling his lounging visitors that gunboats being "jist 'round de p'int," he was sending his family out of harm's way, when some one casually remarked, "What you going to do with the Captain? He can't stay here, a paroled soldier, and he can't go with those young girls that way." "By gracious!" Marse Green had not thought of that. The Captain must marry Fanny right away, or run the risk of being captured, for he had no place to go. In pursuance of that sudden plan, an emissary was dispatched to summon me, and to get the Methodist preacher. Messengers were also sent with flying feet among the few near neighbors, asking their presence that afternoon, while Marse Green himself rushed back home to announce the decision to his family.

I arrived in a scene of confusion beyond words to express. Already some kindly neighbors were there helping the distracted girls to pack. Trunks, boxes, bags, barrels, baskets, were in every room with piles and piles of household and personal articles to be stowed. Everybody was busy and everybody stumbling and tearing about in every other body's way. Marse Green had already descended upon them with his ultimatum, and worse became the confusion with this new and unexpected element injected into it. Dear Fanny must be married in white, so every one declared. Then ensued a ransacking of trunks and drawers for a pretty white lawn she had—somewhere! At length it was brought to light in a very crumpled condition, not having been worn since the winter (the last Buchanan winter) Fanny spent in Washington with her father. There was no time or opportunity or place, apparently, to press the wrinkles out and make the really handsome gown presentable. Then there arose a clamor and frantic search for white stockings. Nobody had the temerity to mention white kid gloves. They were of the past, as completely as a thousand other necessities we had learned to do without. The black dress was laid aside. Fanny looked very lovely in her white gown, the most calm and composed of any of us.

The dazed, bewildered and half-sick Captain meandered around in his dingy Confederate gray, the only suit he had. His skull had been fractured in battle (I think at Shiloh), the hair had been shaved off one side of his head and a silver plate covered and protected the wound. Time was passing swifter than the motions of the little party, fast as they were. All the packing and loading of wagons had to be completed for the early morning start. The rest of us could stay in our homes and run our chances—which we did, woe is me!—but Marse Green's girls must be off, in accordance with his dictum, and, of course, a Confederate officer had to get out of the enemy's reach.

Meanwhile the other invited neighbors were arriving, and also an Episcopal minister. Mr. Crenshaw, the Methodist preacher, could not be found. He had spent hours haranguing the few peace-loving Jews, superannuated cripples and handful of "Druthers" remaining in town, telling those incapables or insufficients they were not patriotic to

stand aside and let the enemy's gunboats land at
our wharf, but it appears when the latter really were
"just behind de p'int," the voluble gentleman's discretion got the better of his valor, and he had in-
gloriously fled.

One kindly neighbor, a late arrival, whispered to
another, who had been there all day helping, "Any
refreshments?" Not a soul had thought of refreshments; we isolated housekeepers had not even heard
the name for so long that it had not occurred to us
to talk of furnishing what we could not procure.
The late comer rushed home and quickly returned
with the half of a cornmeal pound-cake and a pitcher
of brown sugar lemonade. Then the minister required some one to give the bride away. That was
not in Marse Green's Methodist service, and besides Marse Green was getting mortally tired and
fractious, so, without my knowing it, Mr. McHatton
volunteered to perform that function. We guests
who had been behind the scenes, and were getting
to be mortally tired and fractious, too, assembled in
the hastily-cleared parlor to witness the ceremony.

I was struck with amazement to see my husband,
who had been the busiest man there all day, march
into the room with dear, pretty Fanny on his arm!
I never did know where the necessary ring came
from, but somebody produced a plain gold ring,

which, no doubt, was afterwards returned with appropriate thanks. The Captain was a strikingly handsome man, even with a bandaged head and those ill-fitting clothes, not even store-made, and we all agreed Fanny looked very placid and happy. Their healths were drunk in tepid lemonade (did you ever drink brown sugar lemonade? If your grandmother is a Southern woman I'll be bound she has). There was a hurried "God bless you!" and a kiss, and I had to rush home to two wounded brothers needing my care.

Some near neighbors stayed to assist in the further preparations for an early flight. I afterwards heard the entire family, groom and all, were at work all night, and at early dawn Marse Green was able to start the loaded wagons to the piny, sandy country. The bride and groom and two young sisters piled into the ramshackle old family carriage, and were driven off, a ten hours' trip to Amite. I trust they made it before night, but it was many years thereafter before I knew anything further of them.

I asked my husband, afterwards, when we talked the wedding over, who paid the minister? We had not seen yet a Confederate soldier with as much money as a wedding fee in his pocket. "I don't think the Captain had a dollar," he replied, "so I whispered him to be easy; we would attend to the minister." No hat was passed around, but someone produced a fifty-dollar Confederate bill—unless it was parted with very promptly it was not worth fifty cents to the preacher.

The gunboats the frantic negroes had so long heralded, got "round de p'int" at last, and a battle ensued in the very streets of our town. Marse Green's house happened to be in the thick of it, and consequently was so riddled that it was put permanently out of commission. The family never returned to it, even to view the ruins.

At the time of the exposition I accidentally met the Captain and his wife on a street car in New Orleans. At Napoleon avenue the car stopped and the passengers were leaving. I asked in a general way, knowing no one, "Do we change cars here?" A voice, whose owner was out of sight, promptly replied, "Yes, madam, you wait for me." I was thus the last passenger to descend, and to my unspeakable amazement I was received by the Captain and Fanny! She said, though she did not see me, she had recognized my voice, and she reminded me that it was almost twenty-one years since we parted. It was sweet to know that the marriage in haste had not the proverbial sequel of repentance at leisure. They were a happy couple.

The whole wedding affair was a painful and pitiful episode, and for years I had thought of it with
a tinge of sadness; but a few years ago, on a later
visit to New Orleans, I had the happiness to meet
a dear old friend who was one of the busiest helpers
on the occasion, and we merrily laughed over the recalled incidents that at the time were so pathetic.
The handsome Captain may be living; I have since
lost track of him, but every other soul that was at
that wedding has gone where there's no marrying
or giving in marriage—I, only, am left to chronicle
this wedding in war-time.

XXXIV

SUBSTITUTES

MRS. WALKER sent me a pan of flour! It was the first time in months and almost the last time in years that I saw flour. These, you must know, were war times, and flour was not the only necessary we lacked. Dear Dr. Stone had a bluff, hearty way of arriving at things. When the Federals were in New Orleans he was often called for a surgical consultation, or to administer to an officer, with headache or backache, for they were mortally afraid of yellow fever, and it was just the season for it; and their regimental surgeons were not familiar with the scourge. Dr. Stone frequently "made a bargain" before he would act, and so I do not doubt in that way he obtained permission to ship a barrel of flour—for which all of us were famishing—to Mrs. Stone's sister on the coast. Mrs. Walker most generously shared it with her neighbors.

Indians had lived on cornmeal and prospered therewith. Negroes had lived on cornmeal and prospered also. We were living on cornmeal and not prospering, for we had been brought up on (metaphorically speaking) nectar and ambrosia. Our cakes even, everybody had to have cakes! were made of cornmeal and molasses. . . . But I want to tell more about our Dr. Stone. When one Northern officer sent for him to consult about amputating a leg the doctor told him, in his blunt, positive way, he would not even examine the wounded member until he had in his pocket a permit for Mrs. Stone and the ladies associated with her to visit the Parish Prison and minister to the Confederates confined there. It was the only time any of us ever heard of a body asking the privilege of entering that dirty old calaboose down by Congo Square.

Many such stories were wafted to us about Dr. Stone. Some may not have been authentic, but we loved to hear and to repeat them. However, after the war, I did hear him tell of a Union officer offering him the present of a fine horse in recognition of some professional obligation. "I needed that horse," he said, "for I had none, and so I was going my rounds a-foot, but it was branded U. S. and I returned it." Years after I met that Federal officer in St. Paul, and, speaking of the doctor, whom he admired greatly, he told of the horse he had tendered him, which was promptly returned, accompanied with a most amusing note, ending with "So US don't want that horse."

Every blessed one of us was a coffee drinker, and even before the secession of Louisiana we were weighing and measuring what coffee we had on hand, not knowing where we could replenish our diminishing stock. Gov. Manning, of South Carolina, and his wife were our guests at this crisis, and Mrs. Manning showed me how to prepare a substitute for coffee. Gracious me! that was the first, but we had substitutes for almost every article, both to eat and to wear, before we were whipped like naughty children and dragged back into the Union, and made to take our nauseous medicine, labeled "Reconstruction." And now we are all cured! and will never be naughty again.

That first substitute, which was followed by a score of others, was sweet potatoes, cut, dried, toasted, ground and boiled. The concoction did not taste so very bad, but it had no aroma, and, of course, no exhilarating quality; it was simply a sweety, hot drink. We had lots of Confederate money, but it quickly lost any purchasing power it ever had. There was nothing for sale, and we could not have bought anything even if shops had been stocked with goods and supplies. A pin! Why to this day I always stoop to pick up a pin, I learned so to value that insignificant necessary in the days we could not buy a pin. A hairpin! Many women in country towns used thorns to secure their "waterfalls." We wore waterfalls; chignons they were called later. I saw many of them made of silk strings, plaited or twisted. Women had to be in the fashion, as Dr. Talmage once said, "though the heavens fell." If we had had anything to sew we would have missed the usual needle supply.

I was visiting one day when one large and one small needle were all there were in the house; if they had been made entirely of gold, instead of "gold-eyed" only, they could not have been more cherished. I can hear the wailing voice now, inquiring, "Where is the needle?"

You may smile now at the idea of a substitute for a toothbrush, but, my dear, that oft-quoted mother of invention taught us an althea switch made a fairly good toothbrush; of course, it was both scratchy and stiff, but we never found a better substitute for the necessary article. As for tea, we Southerners have never been addicted to the tea habit; however, we soon became disgusted with the various coffee substitutes. We tried to vary our beverages with draughts of catnip tea, that the darkies always give their babies for colic; and orange leaf tea, that old ladies administered to induce perspiration in cases of chills; and sassafras tea we had drunk years gone by in the spring season to thin the blood. We did not fancy posing as babies or ague cases—the taste of each variety was highly suggestive. I wonder if any lady of to-day ever saw a saucer of home-made soft soap on her washstand? After using it one had to grease (no use saying oil, for it was generally mutton tallow) the hands to prevent the skin cracking. I never used that soap, but traveling in out-of-the-way roads I saw it on many a stand. Clothes, too, wore out, as is their nature, and the kind we were used to wearing were not of the lasting variety like osnaburgs and linseys.

Quite early in the war Cuthbert Slocomb and De Choiseul stopped over a night with us on their way to the front. With them was another young man whose name escapes me now, who was suffering from chills, so he remained a few days as our guest. We dosed him with orange-leaf tea, which was about the best we could do, having no quinine on hand. In his kit he had a lot of chamois skins, which he laid out before me with the modest request I make a pair of pantaloons out of them. We talked the project over and decided overalls were the only thing in that line that could be made of chamois skins, that, of course, had to be pieced lengthways, crossways and sideways. The result was satisfactory, and the young man proudly carried off his overalls. I hoped, but did not expect, that he would escape a rain or two on his expedition clad in chamois skins! However, I was amply repaid for my ingenuity and skill, for I had scraps enough of the skins left me to supply tobacco pouches and gloves to lots of soldier friends thereafter.

At one time, in dire need, I paid one dollar a yard for thin coarse muslin, white with black dots, which looked distressingly bad after a wetting or two, but my crowning extravagance was paying thirty dollars a yard for common blue denim; that was in Houston. Thus went the last of my Confederate money. After that for a while we did without things.

Mr. James Phelps of New Orleans—scores of us must remember genial Jim Phelps—made a call on me in Texas, introducing himself with the whimsical remark that I must look at him from shoulder up and not down, for he had on a brand new paper collar, and had borrowed the use of a razor, and was now out making ceremonious calls! Oh, dear me! we lived through all of these privations, and the few remaining survivors are not afflicted with

nervous prostration, or any of the fashionable ills
of the day. Their nerves were strengthened, their
spirits brightened. They bravely bore the fires of
trouble and privation that make them placidly content with the comforts and solaces of their declining
years.

XXXV

SINCE there are still living descendants of the persons concerned in this incident, I have omitted names. The story is entirely true and well known to many old residents of New Orleans.

More than sixty-five years ago, a man I shall not name, was tried and convicted of fraud against the State Land office. He was in the prime of life, educated, a West Point graduate, of good parentage, splendid physique, gracious though a trifle pompous and self-asserting in manner and of presumed wealth. Of course, his case, when it came to trial, was bravely contested inch by inch. Rich relatives, influential friends, and the best legal talent were enlisted, but it was too plain a case of fraud. So, after tedious trial, conviction and sentence to the Penitentiary at Baton Rouge resulted. There were the usual delays, a stay of sentence, a wrangle as to final commitment, a question of length of sentence. His sureties were caught in the net, and tremendous efforts they made to dodge liability for the amount of the bond. Two of the sureties did escape, but the third made good. In steamboat parlance, he "went to the clerk's office and settled."

Meanwhile the convicted man—he was called "Colonel," not by courtesy only, for, unlike most Southern Colonels of that date, he had had military training and might have been even more if he had waited till Generals were in dire demand in Dixie—the Colonel was behind bars in the Parish Prison. The horrid old calaboose down by Congo

THE CALABOOSE.

Square, where more than one Confederate languished two decades later, when the prison was twenty years older and forty years dirtier. The Colonel's devoted wife, who had worn out the energies of a dozen wives, and was still alert and active in behalf of her unfortunate mate, never relaxed her vigilance. When the coils of the law wrapped tighter and tighter around the doomed man, she rose to every emergency. No personal appeals, nothing her fertile mind had suggested, had availed to stay the process of the law. Now that worse had come to the worst, and the Colonel was under lock and key, awaiting the final decision as to length of sentence, Madam and the Colonel's oldest daughter (her step-daughter, by the way) went daily to the calaboose to visit the prisoner. Their visits were made always in the afternoon. The two cloaked and heavily veiled ladies remained till the closing of the gates.

It was in the fall of the year, and election times, when politics were rife. Madam was not only bright and intelligent, but endowed with remarkable tact, and brim full of schemes and resources. At every visit she stopped at the gate and had converse with the warden or turnkey, or whoever was on duty, and related to him the latest news and political gossip and bantered him on his political bias, no matter what that bias was. This course she pursued daily and vigorously. The daughter, still in her teens, was a mere figurehead, always heavily veiled and enveloped in a voluminous long coat. With the slightest nod of recognition to "the powers that be," she proceeded rapidly to her father's cell, leaving her mother, so bursting with talk and information that she could neither enter nor depart without first unburdening herself of the latest political news.

One evening, when matters at court were nearing the crisis, the two ladies rushed into prison, almost breathless, they had hurried so! They had had all sorts of detentions. They realized they were late, and would only have a minute, but they could not let the day pass without the customary visit to the Colonel, etc., etc. While madam was endeavoring to explain to the warden the cause of the delay, and tell also some anecdote anent the election which was too good to keep, the quiet young girl proceeded at once to the cell of her father. The turnkey came in sight, significantly rattling his keys, which roused madam to the consciousness that she had not been in to kiss the Colonel good-night, after all. She had been so interested in Mr. Warden, he was so entertaining, and had such queer views and opinions of the candidates, etc., etc. So, to the Colonel she rushed, returning immediately to the gate, where her friend was impatiently waiting to lock up, signal to do so having been given. The dim lamps about Congo Square had been lighted and a darkening November day was fast closing around them. "Lavinia, come, the jailor is waiting to lock up." "Yes, ma," was the reply from the cell. A moment later: "Lavinia, it is getting too dark for us to be out; come at once." "Yes, ma, I'm coming right now." "That girl can't bear to leave her father." As the madam said this, out rushed Lavinia. Her mother caught her arm and both parties darted through the closing gate, with a wave from madam's hand and a "Good-bye, we will be early to-morrow and never keep you waiting again."

The lock-up took his rounds at the usual time to close the cells for the night. The Colonel seemed to be quietly sleeping in his narrow cot, trousers and stockings carelessly thrown upon the chair. The door was securely fastened by the officer.

Next morning, when it was opened, a gruff voice called to the sleeper, who seemed to be stupidly half awake. Miss Lavinia rose from the bed, showing her face to the attendant for the first time in all these weeks. The Colonel, disguised in his daughter's cloak and veil, had flown!

There were no telegraphs, or wireless, nothing, in fact, but nimble legs and more nimble horses to facilitate the frantic search. The bird had flown afar.

Long before the cage door was opened the prisoner was beyond the reach of the long arm of the law. Madam had for weeks been skillfully planning escape, how skillfully, the result proved. She had engaged the services of the captain of a fruit schooner to take a lady passenger on his next trip to Havana. To insure results, she had privately conveyed provisions and necessary articles for the passenger's comfort to the vessel, bribed the captain to secrecy, and it was planned he would give her timely notice when the tides and winds were favorable to raise sail, and put rapidly and silently to sea from Lake Pontchartrain.

He fulfilled his promises so to do.

When the two (supposed) women rushed into the hack awaiting them round the corner from the jail, the driver whipped up his horses and trotted rather faster than usual down the old shell road he had conveyed these ladies more times than he could remember, right from that old corner to the schooner landing.

Years after these events had ceased to be talked of, or even remembered, and the ladies who bore the colonel's name had vanished from Louisiana, from the deck of an incoming steamer in the harbor of Havana my husband was frantically hailed by a stout old gentleman standing in a lighter. The gray-haired man, who did not dare venture into an American vessel, recognized my husband, whom he had slightly known in the days of his prosperity. He was now an exile, a runner for a Cuban hotel. How eagerly and gladly he took possession of us and our belongings; how he piloted us through the narrow streets; how he domiciled us in the best rooms, and how assiduous he was in attention to our comfort, I cannot tell.

A few years thereafter the poor old man, who had one daughter with him to solace his declining years, passed sadly away, and I was summoned from my plantation home to the stricken girl. She tearfully told me the story of his flight, which had never been revealed before, and, together, we turned the leaves of the worn and faded diary he had kept during that exciting voyage to the Spanish Dominion, where there was no extradition treaty to compel his deliverance to his country. In the early days, when there were no telegraphs, no cables, he managed to support his wife and daughters in New York by acting as commercial correspondent for several newspapers, both in New York and New Orleans, and Charleston also, I think; but that business died out, and be gradually became too infirm for any active or sustained occupation.

His death was a blessed release.

XXXVI

CUBAN DAYS IN WAR TIMES

NOT a Confederate who was stranded in Havana in the '60's but can recall with grateful feelings the only hotel there kept by an American woman and kept on American lines. Every Confederate drifted under that roof-tree. If he possessed the wherewithal he paid a round sum for the privilege. If he was out of pocket, and I could name a score who were not only penniless but baggageless, he was quite welcome, well cared for and in several instances clothed! Some, notwithstanding her "positive orders," exposed themselves to night air, when mosquitoes were most in evidence, and came in with headache and yellow fever. They were cared for and nursed back to health. No one knew better than Mrs. Brewer how to manage such cases. I could call the roll of the guests who came— and went, some to Canada, some to Mexico: Gen. and Mrs. Toombs of Georgia, Gen. Magruder, Gen. Fry and his beautiful wife, who was a Micou of Alabama; Commodore Moffitt and Ex-Gov. Moore of

Louisiana; Major Bloomfield and his wife—some of us still remember Bloomfield. He had for years a blank-book and stationery shop in New Orleans. I have one of his books now, a leather-bound ledger. He was in service on somebody's staff. There were some not of the army, but on business bent, blockade running and so on.

My gracious! I can't begin to tell of the crowd that promenaded the galleries and *azotea* of Hotel Cubano toward the end of the war. They all talked and talked fight, the ex-army men declaring they would not return to their homes with sheathed swords. Alas! They did, though. Before their talks came to an end the Confederacy did. J. P. Benjamin arrived on a sailboat with Gen. Breckinridge. They were wise as owls and had nothing to say. I remember the news came of the assassination of President Lincoln while a large party of the braves were dining at our house—on the *cerro* of Havana. Some of them were jubilant, but a quiet word from Gen. Breckinridge: "Gentlemen, the South has lost its best friend," and a quieter word from Mr. Benjamin: "We will let the painful subject drop," acted as a quietus for our boisterous guests. . . . .

But I must not wander from our hostess of Hotel Cubano. A strange mixture was she of parsimony and prodigality, vindictiveness and gratitude, a grand woman withal, capable of doing heroic things. She knew intimately and had entertained the family of Pierre Soulé, who tarried at the Cubano en route to Spain, when Soulé was minister. The Slidells also were her friends, Jeff Davis' family and scores of other prominent people. She made the first donation of $500 to the Jefferson Davis Monument Association. With vigorous, watchful management she accumulated a large fortune in Havana, though she maintained a host of parasites, poor relatives from the States. She had four girls at one time belonging to her kindred who were too poor to educate them. But her business methods were too queer and unconventional for words. She had leased the large hotel long before the war in the United States, for what was, even in those dull days in Havana, considered a low sum, for the chance of making it pay was a trifle against her. She kept it American style—had batter cakes and mince pies— so that, though her prices were, as we say now, "the limit," every refugee and newspaper correspondent who was sick of garlic and crude oil diet, felt he had to live at the American hotel. Havana was then the refuge of defaulters and others of lax business methods, there being no extradition treaty between the United States and Spain.

SOCIAL LIFE IN OLD NEW ORLEANS

In Cuba when you rent a house, you pay by the month, and so long as you meet the payments, you cannot be dispossessed. (I do not know what the law may be now; I write of forty years ago.) Not long after Mrs. Brewer's venture proved a success, the owner tried every possible way to make her throw up the lease. Anyone knowing Mrs. Brewer as I did, could well understand there was no coercing her. She maintained her rights, paying rent with utmost promptness, and when paper currency made its unwelcome advent and was legally declared of equal value with gold, the payments were made in paper. That currency depreciated steadily and so greatly, too, that Mrs. Brewer told me the rent of her basement to the German consulate for storage purposes, which rent she exacted in gold, was, when exchanged for paper currency, sufficient to pay the rent of her entire building. When I remonstrated with her as being unjust, she explained that all the years she had occupied the building the owner refused to make necessary repairs and alterations. She had been compelled to put in modern plumbing, repairs, painting—in fact, everything—at her own expense, and now she was simply reimbursing herself. When she amassed a fortune, tired of the life, she threw up the lease, returned to the United States and a few years ago died at an advanced age. Her previous history is like a "story told by night."

She was the wife of a United States army officer, stationed at Charleston, who eloped with his wife's seamstress. She did not know nor did she take steps to inform herself, where they fled. He had cashed his bank account and gone. In her shameful abandonment she took passage on the first vessel leaving port for foreign lands. She arrived, a young, deserted wife, in Havana, years before I knew her, homeless and friendless, and was removed from the schooner on which she made the voyage from Charleston ill of yellow fever. When she was ready to leave the hospital, it was found not only the small amount of money in her purse, but her jewelry as well, was barely sufficient to pay her expenses. When she recovered, she speedily found work in Havana, sewing in the house of a Spanish *marquesa,* who became deeply interested in the case of the forlorn woman, eventually assisting her in getting an independent start at keeping a boarding house for foreigners in the city who chafed at Cuban cooking.

A proposition had been made to Mrs. Brewer by two or three American refugees to keep house for them, they to furnish everything, but the generous *marquesa* vetoed the plan and offered to finance a better scheme. So Mrs. Brewer rented and furnished a small house, and the men came to her as boarders, thereby placing herself in a more independent position. From that small beginning sprung the largest, best equipped and most expensive—for her charges were exorbitant—hostelry in the island. Meanwhile the kindly *marquesa* went her way gaily in the fashionable wealthy society of Havana, Mrs. Brewer working and managing, toiling and accumulating in her own domain. They rarely met.

When my family went to Cuba it was to escape from war troubles at home. We sought for rest and peace, but it was not long before we felt we may have "jumped from the frying pan into the fire." Rebellion soon became rife on the island. We, being neutrals, had occasional visits from both parties of the guerilla type. The captains-general sent at frequent intervals from the mother country ruled with severity.

One morning while I was visiting Mrs. Brewer, the *marquesa* called, in a terrible state of mind. Her young son, an only child, had been arrested, imprisoned and sentenced to be executed as a rebel sympathizer. She declared to Mrs. Brewer that she and her friends were powerless to do anything in the case, and she implored Mrs. Brewer's assistance. It was grand to see how the American woman responded. "Go to your home, possess your soul in peace, if you *can. I will intercede with the Captain-general." She did, too. As I remember, Mr. Henry Hall was the American consul. A messenger was sent with flying feet to summon him. By the time she had dressed herself in her finest finery and decked her person with all the jewels she could muster and had her carriage and liveried coachman ready, Mr. Hall had put on his official dress, both knowing how important it was to create an impression on the wily Spaniard. They looked as if they might be more than count and countess, marquis and *marquesa* themselves.

Arriving at the palace, our consul obtained immediate access to the potentate. Mrs. Brewer was introduced with a flourish, and she at once proceeded to tell her story. She told of the extreme youth of the prisoner, too immature to be a volunteer on either side, too inexperienced to have any opinion, and so on, imploring him to spare the life of "an only son, and his mother a widow." The stern old man only shook his head and repeated that his orders were absolute and unchangeable. Mrs. Brewer fell upon her knees before him, declaring she would not rise until he at least commuted the sentence to banishment to Spain. She told him her own story; how she, a friendless woman, had been succored and

20   293

comforted and assisted by the boy's mother years before. She had been grateful, but had never had the opportunity to prove the depth of her gratitude.

I was still at Hotel Cubano, waiting, oh, so anxiously, to know the result of the mission, when Mrs. Brewer returned radiant. She had gone from the palace with the sentence of banishment in her hand to the *marquesa's* home. The young boy sailed the following day to Spain. Mr. Hall told me afterwards he had never witnessed such a scene; had never heard such an impassioned appeal. "It would," he said, "have moved an image of stone."

XXXVII

"WE SHALL KNOW EACH OTHER THERE"

D ID you ever hear the old Methodist hymn, "We Shall Know Each Other There"? It appeals to me rather strongly now, when I read a long list of the names of those already "there," who attended a meeting in New Orleans over sixty years ago, in behalf of Gen. Zach Taylor's nomination for the United States Presidency. Every name is familiar to me. Each one calls to mind the features of a friend, and every blessed one of them has long ago joined the immortals. I trust they "know each other there."

Here's the name of Glendy Burke, who promised me a gold thimble when I was a little girl making my first attempt at cross-stitch, if I would finish the footstool for him. I earned the gold thimble, large enough for my finger, long after I was grown and married.

Cuthbert Bullitt and Levi Peirce! It seemed to require the presence of both to make a mass meeting a complete success. They lived almost side by side on St. Charles Street at that time. It was only the other day dear Mrs. Peirce died. She was born in 1812. I loved to visit the Peirces, though the daughters, Cora and Caroline, were at least ten years my senior. They never married, so managed to "keep young," though Caroline was an invalid. She laughingly told me she had rheumatism of the heart and inner coating of the ribs, whatever that may mean.

In 1849 her doctor ordered her to Pass Christian, so early that the hotel, which I have attempted to describe in a previous chapter, was not open for the season. I was invited to accompany the two sisters. At first we were the only guests in the hotel, but presently there arrived J. DeB. De Bow of "Review" fame, and another bachelor, lacking the giddy and frivolous elements, a Mr. De Saulles. Mr. Pierce had sent us forth in style, with a mature maid, as duenna, to look after the three frisky misses, also a pack of cards and a bag of picayunes, to play that elevating and refining game of poker. I never enjoyed an outing more than those two out-of-season weeks at the old hotel at Pass Christian.

The two bachelors did not bother us with attentions, but, strange to say, Mr. De Bow and I actually felt congenial, and after our return to the city he made me several calls, and as the forgetful old lady remarked, "Might have been calling till now," but some busybody—I always had my suspicions who—sent me at New Year's, with Mr. De Bow's card, a gaudily bound volume of "Poems of Amelia," the silliest of love trash. I still have the book; it's of the kind you never can lose. I showed it to him—so innocently, too, and thanked him the best I could for the uncomplimentary present. My old beau never called again. He was sensitive to ridicule, and seemed to have taken it *au sérieux*. . . .

However, all this is a sidetrack. Mr. De Bow was not at that meeting, but Col. Christy and J. A. Maybin were. They were not of the De Bow type, but their familiar names are on the list before me. Both the Christys and Maybins lived near the Strawbridges, way off Poydras Street.

Here's the name of Maunsel White, too. Both he and Christy were colonels—I believe veterans of the battle of New Orleans—the anniversary of which, the 8th of January, is always celebrated on the spot, and nowhere else I ever heard of. I never heard of one of Gen. Jackson's men that was just a plain soldier in the ranks. They all had titles, from Gen. McCausland, who lived near Laurel Hill, down. I was a friend of Col. White's daughter, Clara, and recall a delightful visit I made to their plantation, "Deer Range." It must have been in March, for the dear Irish gentleman had a holiday. All the bells were ringing the day in, when I rose the first morning, and the old gentleman, after singing for our benefit "St. Patrick's Day in the Morning," proclaimed a plantation holiday. It was all great fun.

S. J. Peters I knew after my marriage. He was a lifelong friend of my husband's. As long as he lived, and we were on our plantation, he sent us every New Year's a demijohn of fine Madeira, by that universal express of the day, the *Belle Creole*. I forget how Mr. Peters looked, or anything I ever heard him say, but one does not easily forget a yearly present of five gallons of choice old wine.

Now here's the name of John Hagan. Isn't he the one who used to walk with two canes or a crutch? When I was a little child, of the credulous type, one of our darkies—the one that knew everything— told me "Dat man (speaking of a beggar that hobbled by) walks dat-away, caze he ain't got no toes; you cain't walk lessen you got toes." I visited the Hagans once on their plantation and knew one of the younger sons, James, quite well, but he was the kind of beau that did not dance, and the dancing girls of my day had little use for such. So it is, my mind runs riot over this list, for I knew each name and some incident in the life or doings of each, pops up before me, and sends my thoughts wandering afar.

T. G. Morgan and W. W. McMain must have presented themselves as representing Baton Rouge. Both hailed from there. Besides they may have had a personal interest in the meeting, as Gen. Taylor was temporarily a neighbor, being in command at the Baton Rouge barracks. I wonder if those same barracks was not the only United States military station in Louisiana?

In the beginning of the war we Baton Rouge folks seemed to talk as though it was the only one in the South—talked of holding it against all odds —of never furling that home-made Confederate flag that floated over it. We delighted in those first days in just such bombastic talk. When I say "we" I mean those who remained at home, and fired remarks back and forth anent our invincibility. Very harmless shot, but it served to swell our breasts and make us believe we could conquer the whole Yankee land. However, when a few Yankees were good and ready to march in and demand that United States barracks, nobody said them nay.

My dear father, no doubt, would have helped swell the crowd, but mercifully he had fought his life's battle and had joined a greater crowd where all is peace and rest. Col. John Winthrop was a nomad (doesn't that word stand for a modern globe-trotter?), a lawyer who practiced his profession part of the time, but shut up his office, picked up his amiable wife and skipped off at frequent intervals to the enjoyment of travel and foreign life. They lived when at home in a house on Royal Street, a house with two rooms on each of two stories, which was enough and to spare for two people in those days. The Winthrops entertained a good deal too, in a quiet, sociable way, musicales, card parties and suppers. The last time I saw them was during one of their trips. They were leisurely resting in a quaint hotel in Havana. Now they are in the House of Many Mansions, for the dear Winthrops years ago took the long, final voyage. . . .

But I find I have wandered, like any garrulous old lady, into all the bypaths leading from the great committee meeting. After the nomination of the soldier for the Presidency, an office he neither sought nor desired, and for which he was not fitted, he made a farewell visit to Baton Rouge and his old quarters at the United States barracks, to superintend the removal of his family and personal belongings. Of course, the little city that so loved the brave man was alive with enthusiasm, and rose to the extraordinary emergency of receiving a future Presi-

dent, to the tune of a fine satin-lined coach, a kind of
chariot affair, and four horses! Such a sight was
never seen there before, for there were no circus
parades in those days, and if there had been they
would not have honored small communities only ac-
cessible by river and boat. The modest, reluctant,
great man was transported in this gorgeous affair
back and forth, with the pomp and ceremony so
unwelcome to him.

I did not happen to witness that first turnout, but
I saw the same coach and four years after, a faded
thing; it had been in the old stable at the barracks
for years, where moth did corrupt, if the thieves did
not steal. It was a sight that set all the little negroes flying to the gate to see this coach go lumbering down our river road, William S. Pike, the big
man, the rich man, the banker with a capital B, on
the box. Mr. Pike was Kentucky bred and could
handle the reins of a four-in-hand as well as any
stage driver in the Blue Grass region. He was collecting blankets for our soldiers, and made a
hurried call (the road being long and business pressing) on us, just long enough to take
every blanket we had, and the "winter of our dis-
content" at hand, too; proceeded with grand flourish and crack of whip to Col. Hicky's, Fred Con-
rad's, Gilbert Daigre's, on down, down to William

Walker's at Manchac, taking blankets everywhere. At nightfall the loaded coach was driven again through our gate, and the tired coachman told of great success while refreshing himself with something hot and strengthening. The *Daily Comet* had published repeated appeals for blankets, which met with meager results, but Mr. Pike in his one trip in the old Gen. Taylor moth-eaten, rusty, rattling coach swept up every blanket that could be spared, and no doubt a good many that couldn't. The next call for blankets for our half-frozen men, busy in the mountains of Virginia, found us so desperate and demoralized that we gladly parted with our carpets.

The next time—and I suppose the last—that the coach and four were called into service was when Gen. Breckinridge made the attempt to defeat the Federals in Baton Rouge. Mr. Pike got secret information of the impending assault. The Gen. Taylor chariot—four mules this time, but Mr. Pike at the helm—well packed, tight as blankets, with the Pike family, was driven furiously out of town.

XXXVIII

A RAMBLE THROUGH NEW ORLEANS WITH BRUSH AND EASEL

SEVERAL years ago I visited New Orleans with my artist daughter. She had heard in her New York home so many wonderful and surprising stories of her mother's child-life in the Crescent City that she was possessed with the idea such a fairyland must be a fine sketching field. We, therefore, gladly accepted the hospitality of a dear Creole friend, who let us go and come at all hours, in deference to (I was going to say our, but—) my little girl's own free will. It was indeed a foreign land to her when she opened her eyes to the Creole life, the Creole home, the Creole street. Every old gateway and every tumbledown iron railing was an inspiration to her artistic mind. We spent happy days with brush and easel, wandering about the old French quarter, and the picturesquely dirty back streets.

The very first day in the city happened to be a Sunday. She was up and ready betimes to go

303

to the French Market, where I used to go once in a great while and take coffee at Manette's stall. It was a shock to her to see the ramshackle old market she had heard so much about, and whose praises had been sung to her by her Southern mother. No Manette. No stall where she could have been induced to take a cup of coffee; but a few steps off and a perspective view revealed to her cultivated eye the very sketch she wanted, the very thing she "came all the way to New Orleans for"—and a plan was formulated to go another day when the light would be more favorable.

In our rambles down Royal Street we passed an open corridor, with a view beyond of a blooming bit of *parterre*. She paused to look in. I saw only the bright flowers and the vases covered with vines. She saw only an iron fretwork lamp suspended from the ceiling. Oh! that was too artistic for anything! Did I think the people in that house would permit her to sketch, from the entrance, that long corridor and that wonderful lantern?

At that moment a pretty young girl passed through the shrubbery in the rear. I beckoned her. "Oh, yes, she knew mamma would be so happy." The work was arranged for the following day, when the light would be just right. While my little lady worked I wandered around the corridor. The stairs

304

A Courtyard in the French Quarter.

leading to the living rooms above seemed strangely familiar. It dawned upon me that I had walked years before up those very stairs. The little Creole girl crossed the *parterre* again, and was called to see the finished sketch. It was only a section of the corridor and the wonderful iron lamp. I ventured to inquire if the Bienvenues had not occupied that house in the fifties.

"Yes, indeed, my mamma was a Bienvenue." The child flew upstairs to tell her mamma, and quickly returned with an invitation for us. Mamma desired to see the sketch, and to meet the lady who had visited her elder sisters. My daughter, used to the cold formality of the New York life, was overwhelmed with the Creole cordiality, delighted to hear that the lamp which had attracted her was a real Spanish antique, and had been hanging in the corridor almost a hundred years; delighted to be shown the superb chandeliers in the parlors, almost as old; and to have a cordial invitation to come another day and make a sketch of the little *parterres* and of the rambling balconies in the rear.

We did mean to go again, but so many striking exteriors and interiors caught the eager eye of the maiden with the easel that we did not have time. The very next day that roving eye stole a peep into another enchanting corridor. Behold a wrecked

307

"Behold a Wrecked Fountain."

fountain, long out of commission, with a dilapidated
angel or sylph, or armless figure of some kind, cling-
ing to it.   There was another artistic temptation,
but when she saw a pretty black-eyed girl washing
clothes and playing at the same time with a saucy
parrot it was simply irresistible.   The girl was delighted to pose beside the fountain with Jacko on her
finger.   Her voluble mamma, *en blouse volante,*
stood on the upper gallery and watched the work

and commented, real Creole fashion. It was not a satisfactory bit of painting, but the girl was enraptured to accept it and could not have expressed greater appreciation if it had been a life-size portrait in a gilt frame.

Mamma would be hospitable, would have us see the faded old house, which had been a grand mansion in its day. We saw evidences of that in the very large rooms, the tarnished gilding, and the ample passages and old boudoirs. I think the *blouse volante* woman must have had *chambres garnies,* but we saw no evidence of that. She had the daughter play on the one bit of furniture that amounted to anything, the fine piano, which she did quite charmingly. From the rear gallery we could see the top of the Opera House, and she told us they were *abonnées,* "so her daughter could hear the best music." This was a glimpse of the old Creole life that I was glad my daughter should have.

Wandering down, what to her was "fascinating" St. Anne Street, behold a narrow alleyway, revealing in the rear sunlight a cistern, only a cistern, but that atmospheric effect was alluring. Up went the easel, out came the color box. The street was absolutely deserted, and we felt quite secure of an uninterrupted half hour; but a swarm of gamins came, apparently from the bowels of the earth, and surrounded us. At a critical moment a woman appeared, also from nowhere, and began to sweep diligently the little half-dark alley. She was transferred to the sketch before she knew what was "going on." *"Mais gar! c'est Pauline, oui, c'est Pauline même,"* the little imps declared, as they peered over the artist's shoulder and saw the figure. That final touch broke all attempts at decorum, and we begged a passing man with a walking cane to put the mob to flight.

What a delightful reminder of that visit to New Orleans those unfinished sketches are to us now, a quarter of a century after! The one I like best of all hangs in my own room and brings delightfully to mind the day we went way down Chartres Street to the archbishop's palace. I am not Catholic, and do not remember if it was the beginning or ending of Lent, but a procession of all classes and conditions of the faithful, with all classes and conditions of receptacles, were filing in and out the gateway, getting their annual supply of *eau bénite*. The lame sacristan who dipped out the holy water from pails into the bottles and mugs became so interested in a sketch my daughter was making, and so busy with a rod driving away inquisitive urchins, that he tired of being constantly interrupted by the *eau bénite* crowd, so he shut the door of his room. *"Trop*

"A Queer House Opposite."

tard, c'est fini," he said to some belated, disappointed applicants.

Elise sat inside the gateway and sketched a queer house opposite, gable end to the street, and a balcony way high up that looked like a bird cage hanging from a window, a tiny balcony draped in blooming vines. The sacristan was disappointed that she did not attempt the old convent building, but the perspective from the street did not appeal to the artist, as did that one-sided building that seemed to have turned its back to the street.

When we came in after each day's delightful tramp my dear Creole friend looked over the sketches and told us of places we must not fail to visit—places she and I knew so well, and neither of us had seen for many, many years.

We took an Esplanade Street car, as far as it went, then walked the Bayou road to a rickety bridge, on the further side of which was a quaint little rose-covered hut. To the artist's eye it was an enchanting cottage. It was a fearfully hot day, so we had a quiet half hour; not a soul passed, to pause and look on and question and comment. We had a hot walk back to our mule car, which did not have a fixed schedule of arrivals and departures, and we were fain to accept the shelter of a decent little cabaret. The proprietor came outside and in-

vited us within, and his cordial invitation was reinforced by a bustling Creole wife. How these people surprised Elise! So generous, so unconventional
they were. I added to her surprise by ordering
beer!—the only visible way, it appeared to me, of
repaying their hospitality.

Another day we took a car in a different direction.
When the car stopped—nowhere in particular, just
came to the end of the rails—we walked on down,
into sparse settlements, occasional fields, frequent
crawfish ditches, to the Ursuline Convent, not a
sketching trip this time, but a tour of observation.
We had to tramp quite a bit, dodging now and again
an inquisitive goat, of which my city companion was
mortally afraid, following paths, possibly goat paths.
for they meandered round about quite unnecessarily.

At length we reached the little entrance gate, to
learn it was not visiting day. It was warm, and we
were warmer and very tired. Across the road and
the two inevitable ditches was a kind of lych gate,
I do not know what other name to give it, a covered gateway and benches, where the family who
lived behind the inclosure could take the air, and,
incidentally, a bit of gossip, if they had any congenial neighbors. We felt neighborly just then and
promptly crossed the ditches and narrow roadway
and seated ourselves quite *en famille.*

Presently two young girls we had not seen presented themselves and invited us to enter the house. Upon our declining with suitable thanks, a mother came from the house and a grandmother, and we had to accept the cordial hospitality, with a sneaking feeling we had invited it by appropriating the tempting resting-spot. In the tiny parlor was a life-size, full-length portrait of a Confederate officer in full uniform, Captain Sambola, of the Washington Artillery.

They offered us refreshing *eau sucrée* and had us go to the back gallery to see the pet peacock. *Grandmère* made him show off. *"Tournez, mon beau, tournez un peu,"* and the proud bird turned around and spread his gaudy tail. We still talk of that naïve family and the peacock. The two young girls we saw in the yard had aprons filled with violets which they were gathering for the market. Mamma tossed quite a handful of the fragrant blooms into an Indian basket and presented them to Elise. They showed us a near path to the car, and we realized we had previously lost our way, and made many unnecessary steps, but would gladly have done it all over again to have had that glimpse of Creole life. Nothing I could have told my children would have been so effective as the little experience of the hospitality of the family of that *"Capitaine en Washington Artillerie."*

Our hostess mentioned St. Roch's, and down there

St. Roch.

we went, easel and all. Those mule cars seemed to come to a final halt where there was no stopping place, and we always had to walk quite a bit to "get there," no matter where we were bound. We walked a few blocks and turned a few corners, and most unexpectedly ran into the grounds of the sanctuary. At the gatekeeper's little cottage we bought a candle and a book, I forget what it was about; and a leaden image of Saint Hubert, inscribed *"Preser-*

vez nous du choléra." We seemed to be expected to make the purchases, so we did not wish to disappoint the modest expectation. At a favorable spot the easel was opened, and my little lady proceeded to sketch a few tombstones and the belfry of St. Roch's. A kindly priest wandered toward us to say it was against their rules to allow any sketching on the grounds, but as the work was on the way (and he commended it) she could complete the picture. Thus we strolled about the old city of my day, quite ignoring the beautiful Garden District of which everybody was so proud.

Down went we to see Congo Square and the old calaboose. The first is about to be rechristened (some twenty and something street) and the other has gone off the face of the earth, but old Congo Square was still there, and the calaboose, too, when I took my daughter to see the New Orleans of my day. A man with his pail and long brush was whitewashing trees in the square, and a dark-skinned woman was hanging red rags, probably flannel petticoats, on a railing in front of a house. "How picturesque!" in Elise's eyes. She regretted she had not her brush and colors with her.

A kindly friend escorted us one afternoon over the river to the old Destrihan plantation house, and the enthusiastic young artist, who had learned

317

"Never to leave your pencil and pad in your other pocket," had a famous time sketching the broad stairway and the interior balconies, upon which all the upper chambers opened. The grand Destrihan house of my young lady days was dismantled and practically vacant, so we roamed around that interior gallery in and out those large rooms. I was full of tender memories of the generous family of only (as seemed to me) a few years ago. The lawn that extended to the river, where were always skiffs to take one to the city when Eliza Destrihan was a beauty and a belle, was now cut up into lots and built up in huts, for the accommodation probably of workmen on Barrataria Canal.

Elise wanted to see the houses her mother had occupied. I knew they must be dreadfully run down at the heels, and I knew how I had told my children of the delightful life we had led in them. Now I was afraid my little girl would be disillusioned, and she was! We started on Customhouse Street, and I confess to a shock when I saw tickets reading *"Chambres à louer"* floating from the balcony where my sister used to walk and from whence she made signals or called across the narrow street to Mrs. Duncan Hennen, on the opposite balcony. I obtained permission to enter the broad corridor. It was lumbered up with trunks and theatrical stuff, and my dear father's old law office was filled with a smoking crowd of actors and actresses. It was the eating hall, and the late risers were taking their first meal of the day. We did not go upstairs, but I pointed out to the child my mother's window, where she sat so many, many invalid days, and with a moistened eye turned sadly away from my first New Orleans home.

Wandering up Camp Street, at the corner of Julia, the whole Camp Street side of another and later old home seemed to be a carpenter shop. I wonder what the child thought, as she must have remembered the tales I had told of the dancing parties and dinner parties in that house where Henry Clay and Gen. Gaines, and all sorts of celebrities, were guests from time to time. The side gallery, where dear pa sat and smoked his after-dinner cigar, was all blocked up and covered with boards and carpenters' tools. The Canal Street house, near Camp Street, was clean gone, as completely gone as all the fine people that used to visit it. In its place was some mercantile or bank building. I was too heartsick with the sad knowledge of the mutability of these mundane affairs to care what the new building represented.

XXXIX

A VISIT OF TENDER MEMORIES

IT was the year of the Exposition in New Orleans that I arrived with my little daughter on a visit to a Creole friend. We left the train at the foot of Canal Street, and boarded one of those old-timey mule cars, in which the passenger drops his fare in a box and the driver sits on a stool behind a dashboard, reinforced with a stout facing of sheet iron, and manages his mule, if he can. In our case he couldn't. A lot of excursionists, with gripsacks and useless overcoats, filled the little car. When they had deposited their coins, and the driver had counted them, and we were ready to start, Mr. Mule took "de studs" and refused to proceed. When, urged by calls and whip, he let those husky feet fly against the dashboard, with deafening and startling results, the wherefore of the iron protector was made manifest to us. Suddenly, as if electrified, the mule bounded forth, up crowded Canal Street, with race-horse speed. Our fellow passengers, Eastern men, probably, and ignorant of mule nature, jumped from the rear of that racing car, as fast as they dared. I held on to the scared little girl, for I had not lived on a plantation without having become acquainted with mule tactics. When our steed reached his destination, at the foot of Camp Street, there were no passengers in that car but ourselves.

That was our first acquaintance with the queer transportation facilities of that date, but it was enriched by others before our visit to the Crescent City terminated.

We found our friend, dear Phine, in considerable excitement about a trunk filled with silver, that had been in her keeping awaiting a claimant. The Louisiana State Bank had, until the war, a branch in Baton Rouge, of which William S. Pike was president or manager, and his family, as was the custom, lived "over the bank." At the break up and disorganization of all business, this especial Louisiana State Bank removed its assets (if there were any; assets were an uncertain quantity in those days) to the New Orleans headquarters. All the household effects of the manager's family—the accumulation of years, in garret and closets—were sent to New Orleans, and the Pikes moved there too. After the death of Mr. Pike, the family closed their Camp Street house and went to Canada. Thence a request came to my friend, Phine, whose whole unselfish existence had been spent for the help of others, to pack away personal effects, have the furniture sold, and the house put also on the market.

Looking through boxes and trunks and bundles and barrels, she stumbled upon an old, weatherworn, almost dilapidated trunk, without hasp or lock, but securely tied with bits of strong rope. It was found to be filled with silver, bowls, a tea set and various odd pieces. Not one article bore a mark by which it could be identified, not a scrap of paper—all the pieces were wrapped in rags and securely packed into this apparently unsafe receptacle. Phine knew that this silver did not belong to the family, nor to any friend of the family. The trunk was conveyed to Phine's garret, and she sat down to rack her brain about it. At last it was decided that in the uncertainty and alarm of the early war days, some planter brought that trunk to the bank at Baton Rouge, for safe keeping, using every precaution to avoid suspicion of its valuable contents. Probably it came, tied behind his own buggy. There it had lain for years, nobody now left to give any information regarding it. Phine wrote to Mr. Pike's brother at Shreveport, and he knew naught of it, but he advertised it, with the usual "prove property" clause.

A VISIT OF TENDER MEMORIES

In time, a man answered, stating his wife was a very small child during the war, but she remembered a quantity of family silver had been removed from her father's house. She was now the last remaining one of her family, but she could identify one article in the lot, a unique urn-shaped pitcher, of which she submitted a drawing, from memory. The trunk with its valuable contents had just been dispatched to the woman. . . . .

My little daughter and I took many rambles down into the picturesque parts of the old city. I presume in New York it might be called slumming, but every old crawfish ditch and dirty alley was dear to me. Even the old French cemeteries down Basin Street were full of tender memories. When we went home from such tramps, and Elise told, in her graphic way, of the tumble-down appearance of whole streets that mother was so enthusiastic over, our genial host, Phine's husband, would say, "Why don't you go up St. Charles Avenue? We fixed that up fine to show to visitors." But St. Charles Avenue had no sweet memories for me, it had not existed in my day. We saw St. Charles Avenues every day, at home. We had no old French cemeteries, the inscription on almost every tomb calling forth memories of dear, departed Creole friends.

The old cathedral and its environs had to

have several visits. I had to show my little girl (oh, how reminiscent I was, to be sure!) the very shop whose windows I used to look into, at the beads, corals, shells, etc., from Southern seas. And, my dear, the very man with gold earrings was there, shuffling around with strings of rough coral beads, and conch shells, that very man (so it seemed)—and he was not a day older—that was doing that very thing seventy years ago, when I had to tip-toe to get a good view of that entrancing interior.

In the narrow street by the cathedral we purchased rosaries for our Catholic maids at home. We walked up and down the narrow way, looking for a tiny shop where I had bought, years and years ago, materials and a book of instruction for the making of paper flowers. Roses and jasmines and pinks and honeysuckles were hung in lavish profusion all about my plantation home, and they lent quite a festive charm on wintry, rainy days, when there was not a blooming plant to be had. I was reveling so far into the sweet past that I was almost surprised that the hustling little French woman (of sixty years ago) was not there, behind her stack of paper goods, like the man with the gold earrings, but she wasn't, and the very shop was gone, too.

We sat, to rest, on benches in the old Place

Eliza Ripley

d'Armes. I looked at those Pontalba buildings, that faded, dilapidated, ramshackle row, and remembered how fine and imposing it was, in my day, and how I had wished that father would take one of those elegant houses, where we would be so near the French market, and the shop of beads and shells, and monkeys and parrots.

We strolled up Royal Street, and the little girl saw the house in which the Boufords lived, sixty years ago. The saucy child ventured to remark she always had thought I visited nice people, but they must have lived in shabby houses. I did not notice her comment, but proceeded to point to the balcony where I stood to see a Mardi Gras procession, a frolicsome lot of the festive beaux of the period, and to catch the bonbons and confetti they threw at us from the landeaus and gaily decked wagons. It was long after the Mardi Gras of the thirties, and long, long before the Mardi Gras of to-day, a kind of interregnum, that the young fashionable men were turning into a festival. I recall Mrs. Slocomb's disgust when Cuthbert fell ill of pneumonia, after his exposure that day. Cuthbert Slocomb was chubby and blond, and with bare neck and short sleeves, tied up with baby blue ribbon, a baby cap similarly decorated, he made a very good counterfeit baby, seated, too, in a high chair, with a rattle to play with. The "mamma" had long black ringlets and wore a fashionable bonnet. I have forgotten, if in fact I ever knew, what youth represented the mamma. There were no masks, but the disguises with paint, powder and wigs were sufficient to make them unrecognizable. If Cuthbert Slocomb had not been ill, I probably would not have known the "baby."

A NEW ORLEANS CEMETERY.

During that visit I went to the cemetery Decoration Day. Mind you, I have seen about forty Decoration days, North—but this one in my own Southland, among my own beloved dead, has been the only Decoration Day I have ever seen in a cemetery.

(I wish my feelings were not quite so strong.) Phine and I stood beside the tomb that contains the dust of Gen. Albert Sidney Johnston, a man I had known well, a contemporary and valued friend of my father's, a man whose children and grandchildren were dear to me. We saw the solemn procession file in, and halt a little beyond us. The band played "Nearer, My God, to Thee," and hundreds of voices joined in the musical prayer. I could not sing, I never could, but I could weep, and my eyes were not the only moist ones in the assembly. Such a throng of sober, sad people there was, such a lot of veterans, many in shabby, weather-stained gray, that bore evidence of hard service. . . .

Phine had kept track of the people from whom I had been so long separated that age had obliterated means by which I could recognize them. As a veteran, in the shabby old gray (I felt like taking everyone such by the hand), approached, Phine caught my arm and whispered "Douglas West," and at the same moment his eye met mine with a flash of recognition. I had not seen Douglas for over thirty years. And weren't we glad to meet? on that ground, too, so sacred to both of us. And didn't we meet and meet and talk and talk, many times thereafter, in Phine's dear little parlor on Carondelet Street? Indeed, we did.

Later on, Phine whispered, "You knew that man, I'll tell you who he is after he passes us." A quite tottering, wrinkled, old man passed. I gave him a good stare, shook my head. I did not know, nor think I ever had known him. It was A. B. Cammack—who would have believed it? He was a bachelor in 1850, the time when I thought a man of thirty was an old man. We happened to be fellow passengers on that fashionable A No. 1 steamboat, *Belle Key*. I was a frisky young miss, and Mr. Cammack was, as I say, an old bachelor. He did not know, nor want to know anybody on the boat, but it happened he was introduced to our small party, at the moment of sailing, so we had a reluctant sort of bowing acquaintance for the first day or so. *Broderie Anglaise* was all the rage. Any woman who had time for *frivolité,* as the Creoles called tatting, was busy working eyelets on linen. Of course I had *Broderie,* too. Mr. Cammack gradually thawed, and brought a book to read to me while my fingers flew over the fascinating eyelets. The book, I distinctly remember, was "Aunt Patsy's Scrap Bag," a medley of silly nonsensical stuff, written by a woman so long dead and so stupid while she lived that nobody even hears of her now, but Mr. Cammack was immensely entertaining and witty, and we roared over that volume, and his comments there-

on.   I have often dwelt on that steamboat episode,
but I doubt if it ever gave him a moment's thought.
I really think if it had been like my meeting with
Douglas West we might have had quite a bit of fun,
living again that week on the *Belle Key*. A hearty
laugh, such as we had together, so many years before, might have smoothed some of the wrinkles
from his careworn face, and a few crow's feet out
of mine.   But he never knew, possibly would not
have cared if he had known, that we almost touched
hands in the crowd on that Decoration Day.

On and on we strolled, past a grand monument
to the memory of Dr. Choppin, whom I knew so
well, and loved too, girl fashion, when he was
twenty, and who sailed away, boy fashion, to complete his medical education in Paris. Maybe if we
had met, in the flesh, on that Decoration Day, it
might have been *a la Cammack*. We never did
meet, after that memorable sailing away, but he has
a tender niche in my heart even yet, and I was
pleased to see some loving hand had decorated that
sacred spot.   .   .   .

Phine and I strolled about after the ceremonies
were completed. She had a toy broom and a toy
watering pot in the keeper's cottage, and was reluctant to leave before she had straightened and fresh-
ened the bouquets we had placed on the tombs of

the dead she loved, and swept away the dust, and watered the little grass border again.

A year ago she herself fell asleep and was laid to rest in the lovely cemetery, and with her death the last close tie was broken that bound me to New Orleans.

ELIZA MOORE, tenth of the twelve children of Richard Henry and Betsey Holmes Chinn, was born in Lexington, Kentucky, on the first day of February, 1832.

Three years later Judge Chinn moved his family to New Orleans, where he continued the practice of law until his death in '47.

On August 24, 1852, Eliza Chinn and James Alexander McHatton were married in Lexington, and for ten years thereafter they lived at Arlington plantation on the Mississippi, a few miles below Baton Rouge, leaving hastily in '62, upon the appearance of Federal gunboats at their levee.

During the remainder of the war they lived almost continuously in army ambulances, convoying cotton from Louisiana across Texas to Mexico.

In February, 1865, they went to Cuba, and lived there until the death of Mr. McHatton, owning and operating, with mixed negro and coolie labor, a large sugar plantation—"Desengaño."

After her return to the United States Mrs. Mc-

Hatton was married to Dwight Ripley, July 9, 1873, and the remainder of her life was passed in the North. In 1887 Mrs. Ripley published "From Flag to Flag"—a narrative of her war-time and Cuban experiences, now out of print.

The reminiscences which make up the present volume have been written at intervals during the last three or four years. The final arrangements for their publication were sanctioned by her the day before she passed away—on July 13, 1912, in the eighty-first year of her age.

E. R. N.